the Inviting WORD

A Worship-centered, Lectionary-based Curriculum for Congregations

Learner's Guide for Older Elementary Children

Year 3

United Church Press

Cleveland, Ohio

Thomas E. Dipko	Executive Vice President, United Church Board for Homeland Ministries
Audrey Miller	General Secretary, Division of Education and Publication
Lynne M. Deming	Publisher
Sidney D. Fowler	Editor for Curriculum Resources
Kathleen C. Ackley	Associate Editor for Curriculum Resources
Monitta Lowe	Editorial Assistant
Marjorie Pon	Managing Editor
Kelley Baker	Editorial Assistant
Paul Tuttle	Marketing Director
Linda Peavy	Associate Marketing Director
Madrid Tramble	Production Manager
Martha A. Clark	Art Director
Angela M. Fasciana	Sales and Distribution Manager
Marie Tyson	Order Fulfillment/Inventory Control Manager

Writers

Janet Helme, writer of the lessons for Proper 17 through Proper 29, is associate minister of Karl Road Christian Church (Disciples of Christ) in Columbus, Ohio. She serves as chairperson of the Clergy Spiritual Life Committee for the Christian Church in Ohio.

Deborah Diehl is educator for two congregations: New England Congregational Church in Aurora, Illinois, and First Congregational Church (United Church of Christ) in Downer's Grove, Illinois. She is an accredited church educator in the UCC and wrote the lessons for Advent 1 through Transfiguration Sunday.

Dorlis Glass, a United Methodist, lives with her husband near Dallas, Texas. She ministers to children—her own, her grandchildren, those in the local elementary school where she is a volunteer tutor, and those in her local church. She wrote the lessons for Lent 1 through Easter 7.

Tom Malone is minster of education at the Idlewild Presbyterian Church in Memphis, Tennessee. He wrote the lessons for Pentecost through Proper 10.

Marian Plant, an ordained minister and certified specialist in Christian education in the United Church of Christ, wrote the lessons for Proper 11 through Proper 13. She lives with her husband and two sons in Glen Ellyn, Illinois.

Carol Birkland, writer of the lessons for Proper 14 through Proper 17, is a former director of Christian education. She is currently a professional journalist who lives and works in Cleveland, Ohio.

Editors

Carol Birkland is a former director of Christian education. She is currently a professional journalist who lives and works in Cleveland, Ohio.

Carol A. Wehrheim is a Christian educator who teaches primarily through writing and editing. She lives with her husband, Charles Kuehner, in Princeton, New Jersey.

United Church Press, Cleveland, Ohio 44115
© 1996 by United Church Press

Design:

Kapp & Associates, Cleveland, Ohio

Cover art:

Betty LaDuke, *Oregon: Jason's Journey*, detail, Ashland, Oregon. Used by permission of the artist.

Betty LaDuke, *Oregon: Jason's Journey*, Ashland, Oregon.
Used by permission of the artist.

Welcome

Welcome and Information Sheet

Welcome to *The Inviting Word! The Inviting Word* is designed to help you enter into the wonderful world of the Bible.

Look at the painting called *Oregon: Jason's Journey*. This painting of a boy named Jason was created by his mother. She painted him at the window gazing at a bird that is guiding him toward a light. Jason was about to go on a spiritual journey, much as you. As a learner in *The Inviting Word*, you are about to take a journey through the teachings of the Bible.

What kinds of things are you expecting in the coming year as you attend church? Perhaps you will meet new friends. Maybe you will discover new heroes of faith and learn about their adventures.

You will be invited to open your heart and mind to all the experiences that are waiting for you within these pages.

Please provide the information asked for below. If you need help, ask an adult.

Name ....

Address ....

Phone ....

Birth date ....

School ....

Other family members ....

....

What would you like to do? ....

....

....

What do you like about church? ....

....

....

What are some ways you might like to learn more about the Bible and your faith?

....

....

Contents

Moses, Moses!

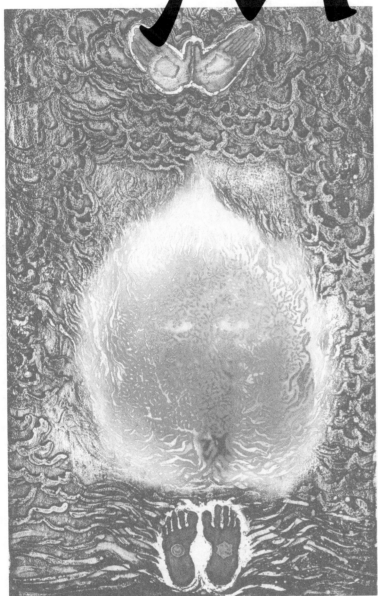

Paul Koli, *The Burning Bush*, as reproduced in *The Bible through Asian Eyes*, ed. Masao Takenaka and Ron O'Grady (Auckland, New Zealand: Pace Publishing in association with the Asian Christian Art Association, 1991). Used by permission.

Moses looked, and the bush was blazing, yet it was not consumed. Then Moses said, "I must turn aside and look at this great sight, and see why the bush is not burned up." When God saw that Moses had turned aside to see, God called to him out of the bush, "Moses, Moses!"

Exodus 3:2b–4a

The colors of this painting are many shades of red, yellow, and gold with black. Hold the learner's guide flat so you can pretend that you are standing on the footprints.

How would you describe your surroundings?

What might Moses or you be saying?

What would you like to ask the artist about this painting?

Thuma Mina
(Send Me Now)

South African traditional song

Leader

1 Thu - ma mi - na.

All

1 Thu - ma mi - na, thu - ma mi - na,
1 Send me, Je - sus, send me, Je - sus,
2 Lead me, Je - sus, lead me, Je - sus,
3 Fill me, Je - sus, fill me, Je - sus,

1–2   3

Thu - ma mi - na, So - man - dla.
Send me, Je - sus, send me
Lead me, Je - sus, lead me
Fill me, Je - sus, fill me

Leader

1 Send me now.
2 Lead me now.
3 Fill me now.

now.

God calls me to...

festival of Freedom

This day shall be a day of remembrance for you. You shall celebrate it as a festival to God.

Exodus 12:14

The Seder Questions:

Youngest child: Why is this night different from any other night?

Leader: In what ways do you find this night different?

Youngest child: I find it different in four ways:

- On this night we eat only *matzo*, unleavened bread.
- On this night we must eat bitter herbs.
- On this night we dip vegetables two times in salt water before we eat them.
- And on this night we recline while we eat at the table.

Meichel Pressman, *The Seder*, 1950, watercolor on paper, gift of Dr. Henry Pressman, The Jewish Museum, New York, N.Y. (Art Resource, N.Y.). Used by permission.

The Jewish *seder* is a meal during which the Jewish people recall that God led them out of slavery in Egypt.

Judging from this painting, what kind of celebration might it be?

Have you ever participated in a meal of remembering? Perhaps a birthday, an anniversary, or communion? Whom or what did you remember?

countdown to Passover

Moses and his brother Aaron meet Pharaoh.
Exodus 5:1-4

Moses and his family return to Egypt
Exodus 4:18-20

The Israelites leave Egypt
Exodus 12:33-41

The Tenth plague: Death of the firstborn in Egyptian families
Exodus 12:29-32

Exodus 7:14-25
The First Plague: Water turned to blood

Exodus 8:1-15
The Second Plague: Frogs

Exodus 8:16-19
The Third Plague: Gnats

Exodus 8:20-32
The Fourth Plague: Flies

Exodus 9:1-7
The Fifth Plague: Livestock die

Exodus 9:8-12
The Sixth Plague: Boils

Exodus 9:13-35
The Seventh Plague: Thunder and hail

Exodus 10:3-20
The Eighth Plague: Locusts

Exodus 10:21-29
The Ninth Plague: Darkness

Exodus 12:1-14
Preparation for the Passover

Adir Hu
God of Might

1 A - dir hu, a - dir hu, yiv-neh vei - to b' - ka - rov, bim - hei - ra
1 God of might, God of right, we would bow be - fore you, sing your praise
2 We en - slaved thus were saved through God's might ap - pear - ing, so we pray

bim - hei - ra b' - ya - mei - nu, b' - ka - rov Eil b' - nei, eil b' - nei,
in these days, cel - e - brate your glo - ry, as we hear year by year,
for the day when we shall be hear - ing free - dom's call reach - ing all,

b'nei veit - cha b' - ka - rov.
free - dom's won - drous sto - ry.
the peo - ple's God re - ver - ing.

From Howard I. Bogot and Robert J. Orkand, *A Children's Haggadah* (New York: Central Conference of American Rabbis, 1994), 70. Used by permission.

Through the Sea

Moses stretched out his hand over the sea. God drove the sea back by a strong east wind all night; the waters were divided. The Israelites went into the sea on dry ground.

Exodus 14:21–22

Find the pillar of cloud in this painting.

Where is the water?

What surprises you about this painting called *The Exodus with the Pillar of Fire*?

What do you like best about it?

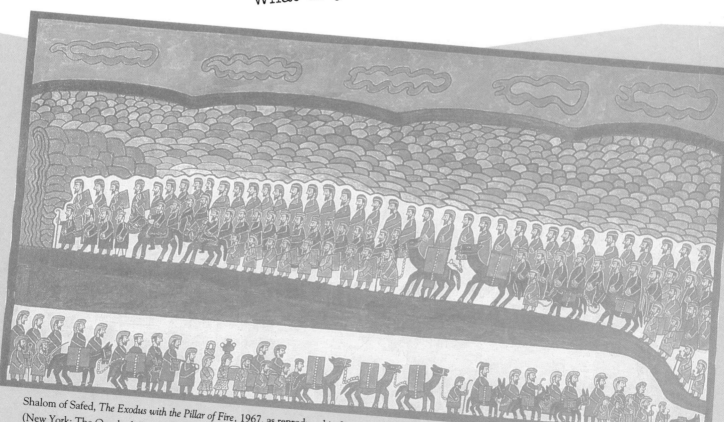

Shalom of Safed, *The Exodus with the Pillar of Fire*, 1967, as reproduced in *Images from the Bible: The Words of Elie Wiesel, the Paintings of Shalom of Safed* (New York: The Overlook Press, 1980), 107. Paintings © 1980 by Shalom of Safed. Used by permission.

Crashing Waters at Creation

Words: Sylvia G. Dunstan, 1991

Tune: STUTTGART 8.7.8.7.; attr. to
Christian F. Witt (1660–1716)

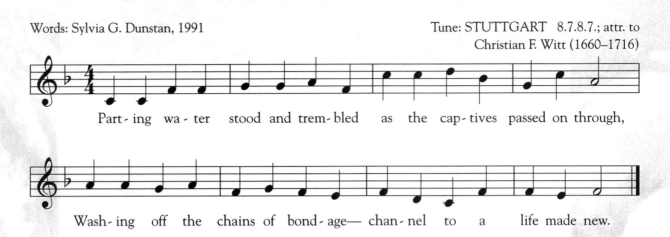

Part-ing wa-ter stood and trem-bled as the cap-tives passed on through,

Wash-ing off the chains of bond-age— chan-nel to a life made new.

RAIN DOWN BREAD

God said to Moses, "I am going to rain bread from heaven for you, and each day the people shall go out and gather enough for that day."

Exodus 16:4a

Moses and Manna from Heaven, stained glass window, Great Malvern Priory, Worcester, Great Britain (Bridgeman/Art Resource, N.Y.). Used by permission.

- This stained glass window is in a church in Worcester, England. How might the time and the surroundings of the artist have affected this work?

- Would you describe this as a happy or sad picture? Why?

- If this were the middle of three windows about the Exodus, what would you expect to see in the first window and in the third window?

God of might, God of right,____ we would bow be - fore you, sing your praise in these days,____ cel - e - brate your glo - ry, as we hear, year by year, free - dom's won - drous sto - ry.

From Howard I. Bogot and Robert J. Orkand, *A Children's Haggadah* (New York: Central Conference of American Rabbis, 1994), 70. Used by permission.

In my dreams, I walk among the ruins
of the old part of town
looking for a bit of stale bread.

My mother and I inhale the fumes of gunpowder.
I imagine it to be the smell of pies, cakes, and kebab.

A shot rings out from a nearby hill. We hurry.
Though it's only nine o'clock, we might by hurrying
toward a grenade marked "ours."

An explosion rings out in the street of dignity.
Many people are wounded—
sisters, brothers, mothers, fathers.

I reach out to touch a trembling, injured hand.
I touch death itself.

Terrified, I realize this is not a dream.
It is just another day in Sarajevo.

Edina, 12 years old, from Sarajevo,
in *I Dream of Peace* (New York: HarperCollins
Publishers, 1994), 47. Used by permission.

for a bit of stale bread.

Käthe Kollwitz, *Germany's Children Are Hungry!* (*Deutschlands Kinder Hungern!*), 1924, lithograph, Rosenwald Collection, National Gallery of Art, Washington, D.C. Used by permission.

TELL the Glorious Deeds

We will not hide them from their children; we will tell to the coming generation the glorious deeds of God.

Psalm 78:4

Jacob Lawrence, *Harriet and the Promised Land* (New York: Windmill Books, 1968). Copyright © 1968, 1993 Jacob Lawrence. Used by permission of Simon and Schuster Books for Young Readers.

Harriet, hear tell
About the Promised Land,
How Moses led the slaves
Over Egypt's sand.

How Pharaoh's heart
Was hard as stone.
How the Lord told Moses
He was not alone.

Jacob Lawrence, *Harriet and the Promised Land* (New York: Windmill Books, 1968). Copyright © 1968, 1993 Jacob Lawrence. Used by permission of Simon and Schuster Books for Young Readers.

Harriet Tubman heard the story of God's glorious deeds and Moses when she was a young slave girl. The story stayed with her. Before all slaves in the United States were freed, she led many of her people to freedom through the Underground Railroad. Her trademark or symbol was the song "Go Down, Moses." Who do you suppose is telling her the story of Moses in this painting?

STORIES can change you.

They can frighten you, tickle you, and teach you.

Stories can be friends for a lifetime.

They can help you make decisions, be brave,

and imagine a wonderful world.

Ainslie Roberts, *The Storyteller*, 1976 as reproduced in *Ainslie Roberts and the Dreamtime* (Richmond, Victoria, South Australia: J.M. Dent Pty, 1988). Used by permission.

WHO TELLS IMPORTANT STORIES TO YOU?

I am the Sovereign your God; you shall have no other gods before me.

Exodus 20:2–3

YOU SHALL

Grade 4 at St. Francis Xavier School, *Moses Quilt*, 1994, 45 West High Street, Gettysburg PA 17325. Used by permission.

Who is the person holding the stone tablet?

Why did the children place this picture in the middle of the quilt?

What stories about Moses do you see in the quilt?

What other stories about Moses do you know?

Worship no god but me.

What or whom do I worship?

What are my gods?

Keep the Sabbath holy.

What do I do now on the Sabbath or Sunday?

What can I do to make my Sabbath holy?

Grade 4 at St. Francis Xavier School, *Moses Quilt,* detail, 1994,
45 West High Street, Gettysburg PA 17325. Used by permission.

Our Prayer of Love

God of Moses and of Sarah and Abraham, God of all love,

We are your children. We belong to you. You love and know each of us by name.

You are always with us. You stand by our side wherever we go and whatever we do.

We promise to try our best to love and to worship you. We will find new ways to make your day of worship a special day.

In Jesus' name we pray. Amen.

Many CALLED, Few CHOSEN

Jesus said, "The dominion of heaven may be compared to a king who gave a wedding banquet for his son. For many are called, but few are chosen."

Matthew 22:2, 14

Diego Rivera, *Dance in Tehuantepec*, 1928, private collection. Courtesy of Sotheby's, New York, N.Y. Used by permission.

Where do you think this dance is taking place?

How do you think the people in this picture are feeling?

What might they be thinking?

If you were invited to this party, what would you do to get ready?

Rembrandt Harmensz van Rijn, *The Parable of the Unworthy Wedding Guest*, Albertina Museum, Vienna, Austria. Used by permission.

What does this picture have to tell us about entering more fully into God's world?

What do you think the man who is standing is saying to the man on the floor?

If you accept an invitation, it could change your life forever.

Leader: God has called and chosen us to live fully in God's world.

People: We ask, O God, that you guide us in knowing how to live fully in your world.

Leader: We shall live fully as we rejoice, as we pray, and as we make our gentleness known to others.

People: We ask, O God, that you help us learn to rejoice, and pray, and be gentle.

Leader: We shall be makers of God's peace and shall look for what is true and just and pleasing to God.

People: We ask, O God, that you fill us with your peace, truth, and justice so that we are pleasing to you.

All: We pray in Jesus' name. Amen.

Based on Philippians 4:4–8

Belonging to God

Titian, *The Tribute Money*, The National Gallery, London, England. Used by permission.

Jesus said to them, "Give therefore to the emperor the things that are the emperor's and to God the things that are God's."

Matthew 22:21

Look carefully at the faces of the people in this picture.
What do you think they might be saying?
What might they be feeling?

Which of the people might be the Herodians? Pharisees?

If you had a chance to talk with the artist Titian,
what would you like to ask him? How is his portrayal
of Jesus different from other paintings of Jesus?

Imagine

Imagine yourself as one of God's coins.

As God's coin, you *belong* to God.

Imagine that God is going to use you in a special way.

How might God use you to help others, to let the world know that you are one of God's coins?

We Are Your People

We are your people: Spirit of grace, you dare to make us Christ to our neighbors of every culture and place.

Joined in community, treasured and fed, may we discover gifts in each other, willing to lead and be led.

Rich in diversity, help us to live closer than neighbors, open to strangers, able to clash and forgive.

Glad of tradition, help us to see in all life's changing, where Christ is leading, where our best efforts should be.

Give, as we venture justice and care (peaceful, insisting, risking, resisting), wisdom to know when and where.

Spirit, unite us, make us, by grace, willing and ready, Christ's living body, loving the whole human race.

At Home with God

God, you have been our dwelling place in all generations.

Psalm 90:1

Charles E. Burchfield,
Six O'Clock, Everson Museum
of Art, Syracuse, N.Y.
Used by permission.

What is happening in this painting?

How does this painting make you feel?

Would you like to live in this home? Why or why not?

All that matters is to be at one with the living God
to be a creature in the house of the God of Life.

Like a cat asleep on a chair
at peace, in peace
and at one with the master of the house, with the mistress,
at home, at home in the house of the living,
sleeping on the hearth, and yawning before the fire.

Sleeping on the hearth of the living world
yawning at home before the fire of life
feeling the presence of the living God
like a great reassurance
a deep calm in the heart
a presence
as of the master sitting at the board
in his own and greater being,
in the house of life.

D. H. Lawrence, "Pax," in *The Complete Poems of D. H. Lawrence*, ed.
Vivian de Sola Pinto and F. Warren Roberts (New York: Viking Press, 1964),
1:153. Copyright © 1964, 1971 by Angelo Ravagli and C.M. Weckley, Executors
of the Estate of Frieda Lawrence Ravagli. Used by permission of Viking Penguin,
a division of Penguin Books USA, Inc.

A Sioux Prayer

. . . Tonight I will sleep beneath your feet, O Lord of the mountains and valleys, ruler of the trees and vines. I will rest in your love, with you protecting me as a father protects his children, with you watching over me as a mother watches over her children. Then tomorrow the sun will rise and I will not know where I am; but I know that you will guide my footsteps.

"A Sioux Prayer," in *The Harper Collins Book of Prayers*, ed. Robert Van de Weyer (San Francisco: HarperSan Francisco, 1993), 322. Used by permission of HarperCollins Publishers, Inc.

You Are Mine

I will come to you in the silence,
I will lift you from all your fear.
You will hear my voice,
I claim you as my choice,
be still and know I am here.

I am hope for all who are hopeless,
I am eyes for all who long to see.
In the shadows of the night,
I will be your light,
come and rest in me.

I am strength for all the despairing,
healing for the ones who dwell in shame.
All the blind will see,
the lame will all run free,
and all will know my name.

I am the Word that leads all to freedom,
I am the peace the world cannot give.
I will call your name,
embrace all your pain,
stand up, now walk, and live!

Refrain:
Do not be afraid I am with you.
I have called you each by name.
Come and follow me,
I will bring you home;
I love you and you are mine.

From Table to Town

Some wandered in desert wastes, finding no way to an inhabited town; hungry and thirsty, their soul fainted within them. God lets the hungry live, and they establish a town to live in.

Psalm 107:4–5, 36

Andrew Wyeth, *Christina's World*, 1948, tempera on gessoed panel, 32 1/4 x 47 3/4", The Museum of Modern Art, New York, N.Y. Purchase. Photograph © 1996, The Museum of Modern Art. Used by permission.

Look at the woman in the picture. Without seeing her face, what about her suggests what she might be feeling?

How does this picture remind you of the verses from Psalm 107 on this page?

What story could you imagine about this picture that would match the verses from Psalm 107 on this page?

Dear God who meets our needs, help us to recognize and see you wherever you may be waiting for us. We may be hungry for many things. We may have a thirst for truth. Fill us with all the things we need.

The ache for home lives in all of us, the safe place where we can go as we are and not be questioned.

Maya Angelou, *All God's Children Need Traveling Shoes*
(New York: Random House, 1986), 83.

Manuscript illumination, *Depiction of a Medieval Town (August: Corn Harvest)*, c. 1500,
Golf Book of Hours, MS. Add 24098, f.25v., British Library, London, England
(Bridgeman/Art Resource, N.Y.). Used by permission.

O send out your light and your truth;
   let them lead me;
let them bring me to your holy hill
   and to your dwelling.
Then I will go to the altar of God,
   to God my exceeding joy;
and I will praise you with the harp,
   O God, my God.

Psalm 43:3–4

What in this painting might remind you of Psalm 107?

Choose This Day

Joshua said, "Choose this day whom you will serve, but as for me and my household, we will serve God."

Joshua 24:15

Gotta **Serve** Somebody

You may be an ambassador to England or France,
You may like to gamble, you might like to dance.
You may be the heavyweight champion of the world,
You might be a socialite with a long string of pearls.
. . .
But you're gonna have to serve somebody, yes, indeed,
You're gonna have to serve somebody.
Well it may be the devil, or it may be the Lord;
But you're gonna have to serve somebody.

Bob Dylan, "Gotta Serve Somebody,"
© 1979 Special Rider Music.
All rights reserved. Used by permission.

Synthia Saint James, *Visions*, Los Angeles, California. Used by permission.

What do you think "you're gonna have to serve somebody" might mean?

If you had the chance, what might you ask Bob Dylan about his poem?

A Joshua of the Future

"We're approaching Zephyr, Captain," said Lt. Commander Rausch.

"Put the ship on cruise orbit, and summon all persons to the Great Hall," ordered Captain Byerly.

As she took the transport shuttle to the Great Hall, the captain thought of all the difficulties the crew and the passengers had endured during these four long, hard years of travel through space. Sometimes the other leaders and she had wondered if they were ever going to reach their destination—Zephyr, a planet located three galaxies away from the Milky Way. Yet, through all the hardships, they had known God's guiding presence. And the long voyage had brought the Christians and the Jews closer together. Both groups had been expelled from their home planet when the majority of the people who lived there had voted that nobody could worship God, on penalty of death. So they left for a place where they would be able—once again—to worship the God of all creation.

As she stepped into the Great Hall, Captain Byerly was met by loud applause, shouting, and whistles. She activated her loudspeaker system by touching the tiny button just below her lower lip.

"We're all excited and thankful that God has led us safely to this place. This planet is not going to be a religious police state. Here persons can worship as they please. We shall guarantee that no one will be forced to leave because they worship God. Therefore, each of you will have to decide whom you shall worship in this place. The crew and I, however, have decided unanimously that we shall worship God. Our first worship service will be held just after we land, on the east side of the ship."

What second chapter would you write for this story?

According to AbiLity

Jesus said, "For it is as if someone, going on a journey, summoned slaves and entrusted property to them. After a long time the master of those slaves came and settled accounts with them."

Matthew 25:14, 19

If you were in this painting, where would you be? Why?

Glen Strock, *Parable of the Talents*, Dixon, N.M.
Used by permission of the artist.

God has given you gifts to care for.

THE
Grain OF Rice

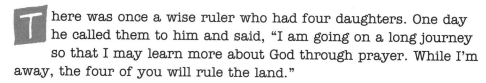

There was once a wise ruler who had four daughters. One day he called them to him and said, "I am going on a long journey so that I may learn more about God through prayer. While I'm away, the four of you will rule the land."

At this, they all cried out, "We don't know how to rule!"

Their father smiled. "I'm giving each of you a gift. I pray that this will help you." Before he left, he placed one grain of rice in each daughter's hand.

The oldest daughter tied a golden thread around her grain of rice and put it in a crystal box. Each day she looked at it.

The next daughter placed her grain of rice in a wooden box, locked it with a key that she kept in her pocket, and put the box under her bed.

"This grain of rice is just like all other grains of rice," said the third daughter. She threw it away.

The youngest daughter took her grain of rice to her room. She thought about it for weeks and months. Then she understood its meaning.

A long time passed, and finally the ruler returned. After greeting his daughters, he asked about their grains of rice.

The oldest daughter brought her rice in the crystal box and gave it to her father. "I tied a golden thread around it and looked at it every day," she said.

"Thank you," said the father, bowing to his daughter.

The second daughter brought her grain of rice and gave it to her father. "I kept this under my bed while you were gone."

Her father bowed to her, accepted the rice, and said, "Thank you, my daughter."

The third daughter ran to the kitchen and brought back a grain of rice. She gave it to her father, who said "Thank you" as he bowed to her.

Quietly, the youngest daughter said, "I do not have my grain of rice. After many months I realized that this grain of rice was a seed, so I planted it. It grew and produced more rice that I also planted. Come and see all the fields of rice that have been feeding the people."

"You have learned what it means to rule wisely," said her father. Taking the crown from his head, he placed it on her head. From that day on, she ruled the land wisely and well.

Traditional folktale

The Least of These

"Truly I tell you, just as you did it to one of the least of these who are members of my family, you did it to me."

Matthew 25:40b

Mona Reeder, *Hau Li Eating Lunch*, as reproduced in *The Daily Republic*, Suisun City, CA, The Best of Photojournalism. Used by permission.

Finding it difficult to adjust to his new school in a new country, Hau Li often eats by himself at Crescent Elementary School.

To which of the groups in Matthew 25:31–46 does Hau Li belong?

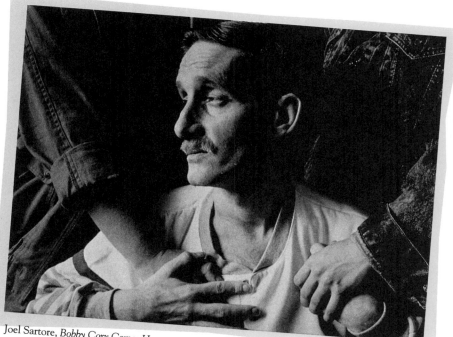

Joel Sartore, *Bobby Cory Comes Home to Wichita*, as reproduced in *The Year in Pictures*, National Press Photographers Association, University of Missouri School of Journalism, 1993. Used by permission.

At thirty-six, Bobby Cory, who has AIDS, comes home to Wichita and support.

To which of the groups in the Matthew passage does Bobby Cory belong?

What would you do for or with them to follow Jesus' teachings to "do it to the least of these"?

Look at the eyes of Hau Li and Bobby Cory. Have you ever seen a picture of Jesus with the same look in his eyes? If so, where was he and what was happening?

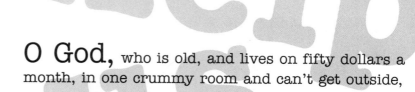

O God, who is old, and lives on fifty dollars a month, in one crummy room and can't get outside,

Help us to see you.

O God, who is fifteen and in the sixth grade,

Help us to see you.

O God, who is three and whose belly aches in hunger,

Help us to see you, as you have seen us in Jesus Christ our Lord.

O God, who sleeps in a bed with your four brothers and sisters, and who cries and no one hears you,

Help us to touch you.

O God, who has no place to sleep tonight except an abandoned car, an alley or deserted building,

Help us to touch you.

. . .

O God, who is fed up with it all and who is determined to do something, who is organizing people for power to change the world,

Help us to join you, as you have joined us in Jesus Christ our Lord. Amen.

Robert W. Castle Jr., "As You Did It to One of the Least of These My Brethren," in *The Wideness of God's Mercy*, ed. Jeffrey W. Rowthorn (Minneapolis: Seabury Press, 1985), 2:164–65. Used by permission.

KEEP AWAKE

"And what I say to you
I say to all: Keep awake."

Mark 13:37

**Who or what
do you think the girl
is watching or waiting for?**

**How does it feel
to wait and watch?**

This prayer is from perhaps the
oldest prayer book, circa 500 C.E.,
of the Western Christian church.

PRAYER Stir up our hearts, we
beseech you, to prepare ourselves
to receive your Son. When he
comes and knocks, may he find us
not sleeping in sin, but awake to
righteousness, ceaselessly rejoicing
in his love. May our hearts and
minds be so purified, that we may
be ready to receive his promise of
eternal life.

The Gelasian Sacramentary in *The HarperCollins
Book of Prayers*, ed. Robert Van de Weyer
(San Francisco: Harper Collins, 1993), 165. Used
by permission of HarperCollins Publishers, Inc.

Salvador Dali, *Girl Standing at the Window*, 1925, Museo d'Arts Contemporanea,
Madrid, Spain (Bridgeman/Art Resource, N.Y.). Used by permission.

KEEP AWAKE,
BE ALWAYS READY

Words: Arthur G. Clyde, 1993

Tune: WACHET AUF, by Philipp Nicolai, 1599

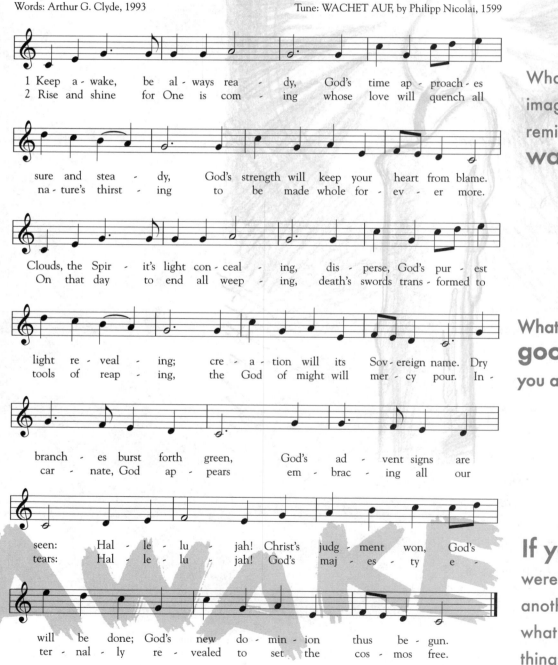

1 Keep a-wake, be al-ways rea - dy, God's time ap-proach-es
2 Rise and shine for One is com - ing whose love will quench all

sure and stea - dy, God's strength will keep your heart from blame.
na-ture's thirst - ing to be made whole for - ev - er more.

Clouds, the Spir - it's light con-ceal - ing, dis - perse, God's pur - est
On that day to end all weep - ing, death's swords trans-formed to

light re - veal - ing; cre - a - tion will its Sov-ereign name. Dry
tools of reap - ing, the God of might will mer - cy pour. In-

branch - es burst forth green, God's ad - vent signs are
car - nate, God ap - pears em - brac - ing all our

seen: Hal - le - lu - jah! Christ's judg - ment won, God's
tears: Hal - le - lu - jah! God's maj - es - ty e -

will be done; God's new do - min - ion thus be - gun.
ter - nal - ly re - vealed to set the cos - mos free.

What are some ways this song reminds you of **Jesus' words** from Mark 13:24 – 37?

What are some images that remind you of **waking** up?

What are the **good things** you are waiting for?

If you were writing another verse, what good things might you include?

Get Ready

"See, I am sending my messenger ahead of you, who will prepare your way; the voice of one crying out in the wilderness: 'Prepare the way of the Sovereign, make straight the Sovereign's paths.'"

Mark 1:2b–3

Pieter Bruegel, the Elder, *Sermon of St. John the Baptist*, 1566, Szépmùvèzeti Múzeum, Budapest, Hungary. Used by permission.

Find **John the Baptist in this painting. How do you know which figure he is?**

What is surprising about the crowd?

If you were among the crowd, where would you be?

 repent,
turn your heart toward God.

What does the word "repent" mean to you?

re • pent \ rē pənt′ \ _____

_____

_____

_____

_____

_____

_____

_____

Pieter Bruegel, the Elder, *Sermon of St. John the Baptist,*
detail, 1566, Szépmùvézeti Mùzeum, Budapest, Hungary.
Used by permission.

Good News Coming

For as the earth brings forth its shoots, and as a garden causes what is sown in it to spring up, so the Sovereign God will cause righteousness and praise to spring up before all nations.

Isaiah 61:11

the amaryllis bulb sends up one shoot that grows so quickly you can almost see it gaining height. Wouldn't it be wonderful if goodness sprang up in our neighborhoods, nations, and world in just that way?

Piet Mondrian, *Red Amaryllis with Blue Background,* c. 1907, watercolor, 18 3/8 x 13", Sidney and Harriet Janis Collection, The Museum of Modern Art, New York, N.Y. Photograph © 1996, The Museum of Modern Art. Used by permission.

Good News

I heard that Jesus is coming. Have no fear!
Amen!
I heard the words of Jesus say the time is near.
Amen!
I heard the Gospel and the Gospel made it clear.
Amen!
Jesus is coming. Jesus is coming. He's almost here!
Amen!
Hallelujah!
Amen!

earth teach me stillness
as the grasses are stilled with light.

earth teach me suffering
as old stones suffer with memory.

earth teach me humility
as blossoms are humble with beginning.

earth teach me caring
as the mother who secures her young.

earth teach me courage
as the tree which stands all alone.

earth teach me limitation
as the ant which crawls on the ground.

earth teach me freedom
as the eagle which soars in the sky.

earth teach me resignation
as the leaves which die in the fall.

earth teach me regeneration
as the seed which rises in the spring.

earth teach me to forget myself
as melted snow forgets its life.

earth teach me to remember kindness
as dry fields weep with rain.

"Ute Prayer," in *Earth Prayers from Around the World*, ed. Elizabeth Roberts and Elias Amidon (San Francisco: HarperSan Francisco, 1990).

righteousness = being upright and good, living as God desires

Greetings, Favored One!

The angel Gabriel came to Mary and said, "Greetings, favored one! God is with you."

Luke 1:28

Paul Gauguin, *Ia Orana Maria (Hail Mary)*, 1951, bequest of Sam A. Lewisohn, Metropolitan Museum of Art, New York, N.Y. All rights reserved. Used by permission.

The artist Paul Gauguin was living in Haiti when he painted this picture of Mary. Who else is in the painting?

How did where he lived affect his painting of these Bible people?

Henry O. Tanner, *The Annunciation*, 1898, W. P. Wilstach Collection,
The Philadelphia Museum of Art, Philadelphia, Pa. Used by permission.

Henry O. Tanner was the son of an African Methodist Episcopal minister. Shortly before he painted this picture of Mary, he had traveled in Egypt and Palestine. He chose to dress Mary in peasant's clothing. What is unusual about his portrayal of Gabriel?

Mary, the mother of Jesus, was from a poor family. How does this photograph of a young woman in Guatemala help you imagine Mary?

Ethan Hubbard, *Young Woman of Costura, Guatemala*,
as reproduced in Ethan Hubbard, *Straight to the Heart: Children
of the World* (Chelsea, Vt.: Craftsbury Common Books, 1992).
Used by permission of the photographer.

How do you see Mary in your imagination? Draw her in this frame.

You are God's favored one!

The WISE Ones

Simeon

God revealed to Simeon that he would not die before seeing God's Messiah. The prophet Anna began to praise God and to speak to everyone about the child.

Luke 2:26, 38

Bystander 1: Hey, what do you know, Simeon's in the temple again today.

Bystander 2: What's new? He's here a lot!

1: Right. Some people call him a wise one, but I wonder. He's always talking about the Messiah, saying that God is going to let him see the Messiah before he dies.

2: God better hurry up then. Simeon's not only a little strange, he's pretty old.

1: Simeon's okay. Just because he's always talking about the Messiah doesn't make him crazy. He's different from some of the others in the Temple. He's holy from the inside out, not just on the outside. When he does good things, it's because he believes in God. He doesn't do good things just for show, like some others I've seen.

2: You're right. Simeon takes God's promises and God's Word seriously.

1: Look, Simeon took that baby right out of the mother's arms! Let's go hear what he's saying.

Simeon: Holy One, now let your servant go in peace; your word has been fulfilled: my own eyes have seen the salvation which you have prepared in the sight of every people: A light to reveal you to the nations and the glory of your people Israel.*

(continued on back)

Rembrandt Harmensz van Rijn, *The Presentation of Christ in the Temple*, detail, c. 1627–28, Kunsthalle, Hamburg, Germany. Used by permission.

1: Shh, listen.

Simeon: This child is destined to be the cause of ruin and recovery for many in Israel. God will work miracles through him. Many will oppose him because of this, revealing their inner thoughts. You too will feel great pain.

1: Do you think that baby is really the Messiah?

2: Simeon seems to think so.

*Luke 2:29–32, translation from International Consultation on English Texts, 1975.

Bystander 1: Look at Anna. She is really excited. What's she saying? Can you hear her?

Bystander 2: I don't know what she's saying this time. People call her a wise one, a prophet, but I've never heard of any of her prophecies being fulfilled.

1: I haven't either. She spends all her time in the Temple since her husband died, and that was over fifty years ago. She fasts and prays day and night. Her prophecies are probably just the ramblings of an old woman.

2: She's pointing to the baby that Simeon was holding. Whatever she's saying must be special because the people are stopping to listen today. Let's get closer.

1: She's praising God for the baby. She is talking to the people who have been looking for Jerusalem to be redeemed. What does she mean? Saved by a baby?

Rembrandt Harmensz van Rijn, *The Presentation of Christ in the Temple*, detail, c. 1627–28, Kunsthalle, Hamburg, Germany (Kavaler/Art Resource, N.Y.). Used by permission.

How remarkable, how beyond the bounds of ordinary possibility, that two old people would see a small baby and recognize that he was the Light of the World! Was it perhaps because they were so old, so near to the Beyond, that they were able to see what people caught up in the cares of life could not see?

Madeleine L'Engle, *The Glorious Impossible* (New York: Simon and Schuster, 1990), 7.

Child, Full of Grace

John Giuliani, *Hopi Mother and Child*, Bridge Building Images, Burlington, Vt. Used by permission.

For the law was given through Moses; grace and truth came through Jesus Christ.

John 1:17

look at the way the artist filled the canvas in this painting.

See how this mother holds the hands of her child. How do you think she feels about him?

Because of Christ, we too can experience God's grace and truth.

Look at this painting. Pretend that the mother is God and you are the child.

How might it feel to be a child so close to God's grace and truth?

Litany

In the beginning was the Word,
and the Word was God,
and came to live with us.
We have seen God's glory.
We have seen God's grace.
God's only child, Jesus our Savior,
    is God's greatest gift.
God sent Jesus to show us grace.
All: Hallelujah! Praise God for the best gift of all.

logos

(Greek)

Both the act of speaking and the thing spoken. In John 1 it refers to the Christ before Jesus was born of Mary.

An English word for logos might be

_____.

CHARIS

(Greek)

To rejoice, particularly that which causes joy, pleasure, gratification, favor. A favor done without expectation of return; the absolutely free expression of the loving kindness of God to humankind, unearned and unmerited favor.

An English word for CHARIS might be

_____.

aletheia

(Greek)

Truth, reality. The uncovered reality that agrees with an appearance. Reality made clear.

An English word for aletheia might be

_____.

Betty LaDuke, *Oregon: Jason's Journey*, Ashland, Oregon. Used by permission of the artist.

And the logos became flesh and lived among us, and we have seen the logos' glory, the glory as of a parent's only child, full of aletheia and CHARIS

John 1:14.

You Are My BELOVED

Just as Jesus was coming up out of the water,
a voice came from heaven, "You are my Child,
the Beloved; with you I am well pleased."

Mark 1:10–11

What Ruler Wades
Through Murky Streams
...

Christ gleams with water brown with clay
from land the prophets trod.
Above while heaven's clouds give way
descends the dove of God.

...

Water, River, Spirit, Grace,
sweep over me, sweep over me!
Recarve the depths your fingers traced
in sculpting me.

Thomas H. Troeger, Copyright © 1984; rev. 1993,
Oxford University Press, Inc. Used by permission.

John August Swanson, *The River*, serigraph
© 1987, Los Angeles, California. Used by
permission of the artist.

Crashing Waters of Creation

Cleansing water once at Jordan
closed around the One foretold,
Opened to reveal the glory
ever new and ever old.

Living water, never ending,
quench the thirst and flood the soul.
Well-spring, Source of life eternal,
drench our dryness, make us whole.

Sylvia G. Dunstan, verses 3 and 4, Copyright © 1991
by G. I. A. Publications, Inc. Used by permission.

John August Swanson, *The River*, detail, serigraph © 1987, Los Angeles, California. Used by permission of the artist.

SAY YES TO GOD

The one who created us is waiting for our response to the love that gave us our being. God not only says: "You are my Beloved." God also asks: "Do you love me?" and offers us countless chances to say *"YES."*

Henri Nouwen, *Life of the Beloved: Spiritual Living in a Secular World* (New York: Crossroad, 1993), 106.

Here I Am!

Now God came, calling as before, "Samuel! Samuel!" And Samuel said, "Speak, for your servant is listening."

1 Samuel 3:10

my child, . . . with the ear of your heart.

St. Benedict, sixth century

What about these children suggests that they might be listening for God? How do you get ready to talk with or listen for God? How can you listen with "the ear of your heart"?

If I were listening for God:

I might feel _____ (emotions).

I might do _____ action).

I might be _____ (places).

I might listen for _____ .

I might listen because _____ .

Brother Eric de Saussure, *Samuel's Calling*, as reproduced in *The Taizé Picture Bible* (Lahr/Schwarzwald, Germany: Verlag Ernst Kaufmann GmbH, 1978), 109.
© Ateliers et Presses de Taizé, 71250 Taizé Communauté, France. Used by permission.

As my prayer became more attentive and inward

I had less and less to say.

I finally became completely silent.

I started to listen

—which is even further removed from speaking.

I first thought that praying entailed speaking.

I then learnt that praying is hearing,

not merely being silent.

This is how it is,

To pray does not mean to listen to oneself speaking.

Prayer involves becoming silent,

and being silent,

and waiting until God is heard.

Sören Kierkegaard, as quoted in Joachim Berendt, *The Third Ear* (Shaftsbury, England: Element Books, 1988). Used by permission.

HOW DO YOU THINK SAMUEL MIGHT FEEL IN THIS PICTURE?

The WORD to Jonah

The word of God came to Jonah a second time, saying, "Get up, go to Nineveh, and proclaim the message that I tell you."

Jonah 3:1–2

Confession of Sin

God of all mercy,
We confess before you and each other
that we have been unfaithful to you.
We lack love for our neighbors,
we waste opportunities to do good,
and we look the other way
when you cry out to us in the suffering
of our brothers and sisters in need.
We are sincerely sorry for our sins,
both those we commit deliberately
and those that we allow to overtake us.
We ask your forgiveness
and pray for strength
that we may follow in your way
and love all your people
with that perfect love which casts out all fear;
through Jesus Christ our Redeemer.
Amen.

From *United Church of Christ Book of Worship*
(New York: United Church of Christ Office
for Church Life and Leadership, 1986), 81.
Used by permission.

Howard Finster, *Nineveh (Garden Wall)*, Summerville, Georgia. Used by permission of Finster Folk Art.

- *Known as Paradise Garden,*
- *the former backyard of preacher*
- *and folk artist Howard Finster*
- *celebrates the primary relationship between God and humanity. On a wall, Finster portrays the repentant Ninevites.*

REPENT!

PROCLAIM!

REJOICE!

God rejoices when we, like Jonah and Nineveh, repent and ask forgiveness!

The Nineveh Times

Headline _____

(Who? What? When? Where? Why?)

Jonah Lost at Sea!

Sailors recently returned from Tarshish reported that Jonah, son of Amittai (a-MITT-eye), was thrown overboard during a violent storm in order to save the ship. Before going overboard Jonah told the sailors that he blamed the storm on his attempt to flee from God. Jonah stated, "God is angry because I refused to go to Nineveh."

Jonah had been asleep during the beginning of the storm and was not aware of the danger to the ship until the captain awakened him. When questioned, Jonah explained that he was a Hebrew and that he was running away from the God of his people. He suggested that the sailors throw him overboard to save the ship. The sailors tried to save the ship without throwing Jonah overboard, but, in the end, they did as Jonah suggested. The storm immediately calmed and they were able to make their way to port.

Some sailors cautiously stated that Jonah was last seen being swallowed by a large fish. This statement has not been confirmed. There has been no further word from Jonah.

Paul Kittelson and Olin Calk, _Whale_, steel and window screen, Houston, Texas. Used by permission of the artists.

What would it look like inside the great fish?
What would it smell like?
What would it feel like?
What would you want to say to God?

A New Teaching

Jesus commands even the unclean spirits, and they obey him.

Mark 1:27

Edvard Munch, *The Scream*, Nasjonalgalleriet, Oslo, Norway. Used by permission.

And the unclean spirit, convulsing him and crying with a loud voice, came out of him.

Mark 1:26

What might an unclean spirit or fear look like?

Psalm 111

Praise God.
I will give thanks to God with my whole heart.
Great are God's works,
God's righteousness is forever.
God provides food for those who fear God.
God remember's God's covenant.
God sent redemption to the people.
God has commanded that the covenant is forever.
All: The fear of God is the beginning of wisdom. Praise God.

Paraphrase of Psalm 111:1, 3, 5, 9, 10a

Have you ever thought about racism?

Racism is something that is not so nice. It is when someone makes fun of you if you're a different colour or if your eyes are different. I never really thought of it until today. Now let me tell you a little story. I tell when I was only three years old mom and dad decided to go to Canada. My sister and I thought it was going to be fun. Naturally we went to the nearest school. I walked into the classroom. It was frightening for me. Everyone stared. The next day everyone started to call me names. I was deeply hurt. It took me a few years to adjust but today I am doing just fine. So the next time you got to call somebody names because they are different from everyone else, think about my story. I know that person will appreciate it.

Mary Hong, age 10, Canada, as quoted in *My World Peace: Thoughts and Illustrations from the Children of all Nations*, ed. Richard and Helen Exley (Lincolnwood, Ill.: Passport Books, 1985), 71. Used by permission.

Who were these scribes?

A scribe was an administrative officer often concerned with finance and policy. He was trained as an expert in the Law of Moses. The scribes often opposed the teachings and actions of Jesus that they thought were against Jewish law. Because they were experts on Jewish life, scribes were often advisors to the chief priests. The scribes in Jerusalem held important offices, but there were also scribes in the villages and towns in the country. The authority of the scribes was based on their study and training as scholars of the Bible.

with WiNGS like EaGLeS

God gives power to the faint,

and strengthens the powerless.

Isaiah 40:29

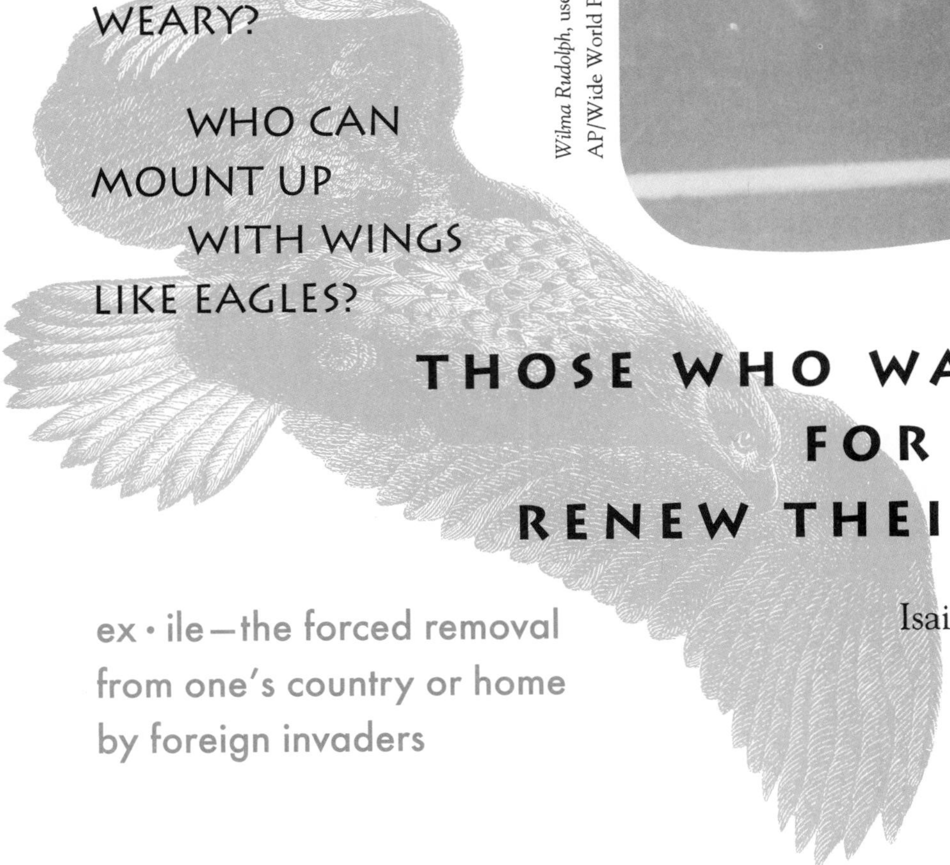

Wilma Rudolph, used by permission of AP/Wide World Photos, New York, N.Y.

WHO CAN
RUN AND NOT BE
WEARY?

WHO CAN
MOUNT UP
WITH WINGS
LIKE EAGLES?

THOSE WHO WAIT
FOR GOD SHALL
RENEW THEIR STRENGTH.

Isaiah 40:31

ex · ile—the forced removal
from one's country or home
by foreign invaders

Isaiah 40:21–31

A Choral Reading

1: Have you not known? Have you not heard?

2: Have you not known? Have you not heard?

1: Has it not been told you from the beginning? Have you not understood from the beginnings of the earth?

2: Our God is the everlasting God, the Creator of the ends of the earth.

1: It is God who sits above the circle of the earth and its people are like grasshoppers.

2: It is God who stretches out the heavens like a curtain and spreads them like a tent to live in.

1: Our God is the everlasting God, the Creator of the ends of the earth.

2: It is God who makes the rulers of earth as nothing.

1: They are barely planted,

2: Their stem has just begun to take root in the earth, when God blows upon them,

1: and they wither,

2: dry up,

1: fade away.

Everyone: Our God is the everlasting God, the Creator of the ends of the earth.

2: To whom then will you compare me?

says the Holy One.

1: Who is my equal?

2: Our God is the everlasting God, the Creator of the ends of the earth.

1: Our God does not faint or grow weary.

2: Even youths will faint and be weary and the young will fall exhausted.

1: God gives power to the faint

2: and strengthens the powerless.

1: Our God is the everlasting God, the Creator of the ends of the earth.

2: Those who wait for our God will renew their strength,

1: become revived,

2: refreshed!

1: They will mount up with wings like eagles,

2: soaring,

1: floating.

2: They shall run and not be weary.

1: They shall walk and not faint.

Everyone: Our God is the everlasting God, the Creator of the ends of the earth!

Today, God, help me to let go of my need to do it alone and my belief that I am alone. Help me to tap into Your Divine Power and Presence, and Your resources for love, help, and support that's there for me. Help me know I am loved.

Melanie Beattie, *The Language of Letting Go* (New York: HarperCollins, 1990), 6. Used by permission.

Clothed with Joy

You have taken off my sackcloth and clothed me with joy, so that my soul may praise you and not be silent.

Psalm 30:11b–12a

Can you remember getting all dressed up when you were little?

Perhaps you dressed up for a costume party or to be in a wedding or play.

How do you feel when you change to special clothes?

Imagine being dressed in the somber clothes of mourning and then changing to bright, cheerful clothes.

How might you look and feel differently?

Litany

O God, I asked you for help
and you helped me.
*I will sing your praises,
and give you thanks.*
O God, you know how to make my heart happy,
you know how to make me sing for joy.
*How could I be silent,
when you have given me such joy.*
All: O God, I will give you thanks forever.

Paraphrase of Psalm 30:2, 4, 11, 12

Cathy Wilcox, in *A Proper Little Lady* by Nette Hilton (New York: Orchard Books, 1989). Used by permission of HarperCollins Publishers (Australia) Pty., Ltd.

The women in this photograph are dancing to gather support and to give support to one another. They are fighting for their rights as women in their nation. Perhaps you have been to a pep rally before a school football game where the group did a "snake dance" as part of getting everyone excited about the game so they would cheer the team on. When else might you be "clothed with joy" so that you want to dance?

Women in Namibia Dancing (Afrapix, Impact Visuals, N.Y.). Used by permission.

God has clothed me with joy!

I WILL DO A New Thing

Do not remember the former things, or consider the things of old. I am about to do a new thing; now it springs forth, do you not perceive it? I will make a way in the wilderness and rivers in the desert.

Isaiah 43:18–19

Diary entry: c. 586 B.C.E.

Oh, great! We are under attack again. King Nebuchadnezzar is outside the city walls—and you know what he wants?—he wants us out of here. This old city of Jerusalem will not be able to keep him out. We are lost!

King Zedekiah made a bad decision. We were caught between two strong countries, Egypt and Babylonia, and the king asked for support from Egypt. It was a tough decision. I don't know what I would have done. We are lost!

About 539 B.C.E.

Guess what? Now Babylon is under attack! King Cyrus is the guy leading this war. What will become of us now? Are we to be led even farther away from our beloved Jerusalem?

Later that day

Well you will never believe it, we are going home. Yep, that's right, back to Jerusalem. God is truly gracious. FREEDOM! We will leave Babylon behind forever. God has new plans for us.

Prayer

Dear God, our creator and the renewer of all things, help us to remember your power and goodness. Remind us that we are your dear creations and that you are not done with us yet. Do a new thing in the hearts, minds, and lives of each of us. Amen.

God of the Sparrow God of the Whale

God of the sparrow God of the
w h a l e
God of the swirling stars
How does the creature say Awe
How does the creature say Praise

God the earthquake God of the
s t o r m
God of the trumpet blast
How does the creature cry Woe
How does the creature cry Save

God of the rainbow God of the
c r o s s
God of the empty grave
How does the creature say Grace
How does the creature say Thanks

God of the hungry God of the
s i c k
God of the prodigal
How does the creature say Care
How does the creature say Life

God of the neighbor God of the
f o e
God of the pruning hook
How does the creature say Love
How does the creature say Peace

God of the ages God near at
h a n d
God of the loving heart
How do your children say Joy
How do your children say Home.

Jaroslav J. Vajda, Words Copyright © 1983
by Jaroslav J. Vajda. Used by permission.

Tuesday, 11 April 1944

We have been pointedly reminded that we are in hiding, that we are Jews in chains, chained to one spot, without any rights, but with a thousand duties. . . .

Who has inflicted this upon us? Who has made us Jews different from all other people? Who has allowed us to suffer so terribly up till now?

It is God that has made us as we are, but it will be God, too, who will raise us up again. . . .

Be brave! Let us remain aware of our task and not grumble, a solution will come, God has never deserted our people.

Anne Frank, *The Diary of a Young Girl*
(Garden City, N.Y.: Doubleday & Company, 1967), 227–28.

In Levi's House

As Jesus sat at dinner in Levi's house, many tax collectors and sinners were also sitting with Jesus and the disciples—for there were many who followed him. When the scribes of the Pharisees saw that he was eating with sinners and tax collectors, they said to the disciples, "Why does Jesus eat with tax collectors and sinners?" When Jesus heard this, he said to them, "Those who are well have no need of a physician, but those who are sick; I have come to call not the righteous but sinners."

Mark 2:15–17

John Perceval, *Christ Dining at Young and Jackson's*, detail, 1947, private collection of Helen and Maurice Alther, Melbourne, Australia. Used by permission of the artist.

Jesus included all kinds of people in his circle of friends. He often ate with people who were not included by others. If you were at a meal with Jesus, like the one in this painting, where might you want to be?

Litany

Bless God, O my soul;

All that is in me, bless God's holy name!

Bless God, O my soul;

and don't forget what God has done,

God forgives all your sins,

God heals all diseases.

Bless God and all God's works,

In all places of God's dominion.

All: Bless God, O my soul.

Paraphrase of Psalm 103:1–3, 22

Paolo Veronese, *The Feast at the House of Levi*, Accademia, Venice, Italy (Cameraphoto/Art Resource, N.Y.). Used by permission.

Prayer

People of God,
look about and see the faces of those
we know and love—
neighbors and friends,
sisters and brothers—
a community of kindred hearts.

People of God,
look about and see the faces
of those we hardly know—
strangers, sojourners, forgotten friends,
the ones who need an outstretched hand.

People of God,
Look about you and see all the images
of God assembled here.
In me, in you, in each of us,
God's spirit shines for all to see.
People of God, come.
Let us worship together.

Ann Asper Wilson, "People of God," in
United Church of Christ Book of Worship
(Cleveland, Ohio: United Church of Christ
Office of Church Life and Leadership 1977).
Used by permission.

What might the people at this feast feel about being invited? Might you want to be included here? Why or why not?

Upon a High Mountain

Six days later, Jesus took with him Peter and James and John, and led them up a high mountain apart, by themselves. And he was transfigured before them. Then a cloud overshadowed them, and from the cloud there came a voice, "This is my Child, the Beloved; to this one you shall listen!" Suddenly when they looked around, they saw no one with them any more, but only Jesus.

Mark 9:2, 7–8

Raphael, *Transfiguration*, Pinacoteca, Vatican Museums, Vatican State, Italy (Scala/Art Resource, N.Y.). Used by permission.

They saw Jesus covered with light, as they had never seen him before. Jesus had been transfigured! Jesus was a person, and yet more than a person, the Only Child of God.

Litany

Come to the mountain.
Come to the place where Jesus stands.
Come from your work, from your play, and from your homes.
To the place where Jesus stands.
Come and celebrate the moment of the Transfiguration.
Come and see Jesus, the Christ, the only Child of God.
Come to the mountain to see the Transfigured Christ.

God's only Child!

61

**To be the same,
yet different—
covered in light—
is a transfiguration.**

You Are Mine

I will come to you in the silence,

I will lift you from all your shame.

You will hear my voice,

I claim you as my choice,

be not afraid,

I am with you.

I have called you by name.

Come follow me,

I will bring you home.

I love you and you are mine.

Elijah Pierce, *The Transfiguration*, Columbus Museum of Art, Columbus, Ohio. Used by permission.

Suddenly they saw him the way he was, the way he really was all the time, although they had never seen it before, the glory which blinds the everyday eye and so becomes invisible. This is how he was, radiant, brilliant, carrying joy like a flaming sun in his hands. This is the way he was—is—from the beginning, and we cannot bear it. So he manned himself, came manifest to us; and there on the mountain they saw him, really saw him, saw his light. We all know that if we really see him we die. But isn't that what is required of us? Then, perhaps, we will see each other, too.

Rainbow Promise

What do you know about Noah's ark?

God said, "This is the sign of the covenant that I make between me and you and every living creature that is with you, for all future generations: I have set my bow in the clouds, and it shall be a sign of the covenant between me and the earth."

Genesis 9:12–13

A Prayer from Psalm 25

Teach us your ways.
Make them known to us.
Teach us to live according to your truth.
With faithfulness and love,
God leads all who keep God's covenant
and obey God's commands. Amen.

God of the Sparrow God of the Whale

Words: Jaroslav J. Vajda, 1983

Tune: ROEDER 5.4.6.7.7.
Carl F. Schalk, 1983

Introduction

1 God of the spar-row God of the whale
2 God of the earth-quake God of the storm
3 God of the rain-bow God of the cross
4 God of the hun-gry God of the sick
5 God of the neigh-bor God of the foe
6 God of the a-ges God near at hand

God of the swirl-ing stars   How does the crea-ture say
God of the trum-pet blast   How does the crea-ture cry
God of the emp-ty grave   How does the crea-ture say
God of the prod-i-gal   How does the crea-ture say
God of the prun-ing hook   How does the crea-ture say
God of the lov-ing heart   How do your chil-dren say

1–5

Awe   How does the crea-ture say   Praise
Woe   How does the crea-ture cry   Save
Grace   How does the crea-ture say   Thanks
Care   How does the crea-ture say   Life
Love   How does the crea-ture say   Peace
Joy   How do your chil-dren say

6

Home.

God's

promise

is in the

rainbow

What are some ways to show that a promise or agreement has been made? Write or draw these signs.

An Everlasting Covenant

I will establish my covenant between me and you, and your offspring after you throughout their generations, for an everlasting covenant, to be God to you and to your offspring after you.

Genesis 17:7

God is faithful.

Noah built the ark because he had faith in God. Abram and Sarai left for the Promised Land because they had faith in God. What have you done because you have faith in God?

Covenant
God given.

Hear! Hope! Obey!

I am your God.

Promise

A Blessing Response

Our hearts *rejoice* in *God's* **wonderful works;** we will **praise God** in our **words** and **deeds.** Amen.

Lavon Bayler, *Whispers of God* (New York:
The Pilgrim Press, 1987), 50. Used by permission.

Nada te Turbe
Nothing Can Trouble

Words and music: The Taizé Community, 1991

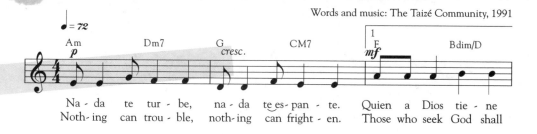

Na - da te tur - be,   na - da te es - pan - te.   Quien a Dios tie - ne
Noth - ing can trou - ble, noth - ing can fright - en. Those who seek God shall

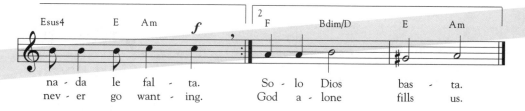

na - da le fal - ta.   So - lo Dios   bas - ta.
nev - er go want - ing.   God a - lone   fills us.

Copyright © 1991 G.I.A. Publications, Inc., U.S. Agents. Used by permission.

over
overturn
the tables

Jesus poured out the coins of the money changers and overturned their tables. Jesus told those who sold animals for sacrifice, "Take these things out of here! Stop making God's house a marketplace!"

John 2:15b–16

It's Time to Change

Sometimes I get so angry!
　　　I yell and hit! I shout bad names!
Sometimes the world gets angry.
　　　Armies fight! Children cry! People die!

Turn over the tables, God.
　　　Help me to be a peacemaker.

Sometimes I'm so selfish.
　　　It's my time! my room! my friend! my stuff!
The people of the world are selfish too.
　　　It's our oil! our fish! our land!

Turn over the tables, God.
　　　Help me to be a peacemaker.
Remind me that everything is yours.

Sometimes I get discouraged!
　　　It's no use! There's no way! I give up!
The governments get discouraged too.
　　　So many homeless and hungry people!
So much disease!

Turn over the tables, God.
　　　Give us courage to try again. Amen.

what's

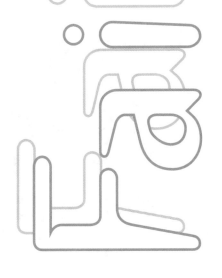

Who is being treated unfairly in each of these pictures?

What could be done to change this unfair scene to a scene where everyone is treated fairly?

What would you do if you walked into this picture?

God So Loved

For God so loved the world that God gave God's only Child, so that everyone who believes in that Child should not perish but have eternal life.

John 3:16

this stained glass window is about freedom, particularly freedom from slavery. As you look at the symbols in the window, which ones do you recognize? Which ones remind you of Jesus?

David Driskell, *West Window*, 1990, Peoples Congregational United Church of Christ, Washington, D.C. Used by permission.

Love Me. Teach Me. Use Me.

Love me, God, that I can better love others.

Teach me, God, that I may teach others what I have been taught.

Use me, God, to do your will. Amen.

John 3:16

(Begin with hands together in front of chest.)

For God so

(Move hands upward and outward, forming two circles.)

loved

(Touch heart with both hands.)

the world

(Move hands in front of body to form circle.)

that God gave

(Open extended hands, palms up.)

God's only Child,

(Cradle a baby.)

so that everyone who believes

(Look up, right hand on heart, left on temple.)

in that Child should not perish

(Bow head.)

but have eternal life.

(Look up, extend hands outward.)

Mev Puleo, Presentation, Brazil, St. Louis, Missouri. Used by permission.

How could this picture help us think about God's love? God loved this world and its people so much that God sent God's only Child to give us eternal life.

The Law Within

Marc Chagall, *Klageleid des Jeremias*. © ARS, New York, N.Y. Used by permission of ARS.

I will put my law within them, and I will write it on their hearts; and I will be their God, and they shall be my people.

Jeremiah 31:33b

A Prayer for Wisdom and Inspiration

Open our hearts and minds, God,

so that as we read the Word

and hear it proclaimed,

we will come to know you better.

Let each story enrich our lives,

each law challenge us,

each song inspire us. Amen.

What is the man in the front of the picture **holding?**

What **can you tell** about him from the picture?

Who else is in the picture?

How do you connect this picture with the **Bible verse** on this page?

Marc Chagall, *Klageleid des Jeremias*, detail. © ARS, New York, N.Y. Used by permission of ARS.

a promise

God's New Covenant

In the days of Jeremiah, the Hebrew people heard,
"You have turned away from God.
You have not obeyed God's commandments!
You didn't pay attention! You didn't listen."

And the Hebrew people prayed,
"Create in me a clean heart, O God,
and put a new and right spirit within me"
(Psalm 51:10).

God's answer came.
"Your sins are forgiven.
Feel the warmth of the new covenant
which I have written on your hearts."

And when we cry,
"I'm lost! I've gone the wrong way!"
The answer comes,
"Turn around! Go the other way! Start again!
You can do it because God is with you."

A Promise

"I'm afraid,"

the little boy sobbed.

"Don't be afraid! I'm here!"

his mother answered.

"We're afraid,"

God's people cried.

"Don't be afraid! I'm here!"

God promised.

Jerusalem

"Hosanna!
Blessed is the
one who comes
in the name
of God!"
Mark 11:9b

Jesus enters the city
and the crowds go wild.
They believe that Jesus
has come to be their
sovereign and ruler.

If you had been
there that day,
where might you
have been?
 in the crowd
that was
shouting?
or with Jesus'
followers?

Litany

Hosanna, hosanna!
Blessed is the one who comes in the name of God.
Hosanna to God! Hosanna in the highest!
Blessed is the one who comes to us from the line of David.
Hosanna, hosanna!
Let the people shout and welcome Jesus into Jerusalem.
All: Hosanna! Blessed is the one who comes in the name of God!

73

Look for symbols to remind you about the triumphal entry of Jesus into Jerusalem. What might some of those symbols be?

A Giant Puzzle

Betty LaDuke, *Guatemala: Procession*, Ashland, Ore. Used by permission of the artist.

This week's a giant puzzle,

    so much to contemplate.

It begins with joy and celebration

    and ends with jeers and hate.

So let's begin our journey.

    Wave branches high and low,

And pause from time to time and ask,

    "What next? Where do we go?"

Jesus Is Risen!

As they entered the tomb, they saw a youth, dressed in a white robe, sitting on the right side; and they were alarmed. But the youth said to them, "Do not be alarmed; you are looking for Jesus of Nazareth, who was crucified. Jesus has been raised, and the body is not here. Look, there is the place they laid the body."

Mark 16:5–6

Frank Wesley, *Easter Morning*, Galloway Collection, as reproduced in Naomi Wray, *Frank Wesley: Exploring Faith with Brush* (Auckland, New Zealand: Pace Publishing, 1993), 38. Used by permission.

A Litany of Celebration

All around us this Easter day
are nature's signs of life and hope.
A butterfly emerges from its cocoon.
Dozens of seeds spill from a pomegranate.
A blade of wheat pushes through the moist spring soil.
A lily blooms after lifeless months of waiting.
Nature remembers the empty tomb and celebrates!
Thank you, God, for these reminders. Amen.

Look at the expressions on the faces of these women.

Do you think they might have heard the good news yet?

2.

Use a pencil to curl petals

3.

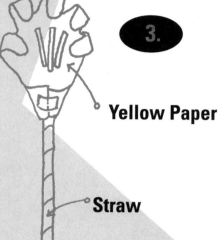

Yellow Paper

Straw

1.

Trace and cut out handprint

Jesus Christ is risen today.

Alleluia!

# of One Heart and Soul

Now the whole group of those who believed were of one heart and soul, and no one claimed private ownership of any possessions. With great power the apostles gave their testimony to the resurrection of the Sovereign Jesus, and great grace was upon them all.

Acts 4:32–33

Faith Ringgold, *Church Picnic*, painted story quilt, Englewood, New Jersey. Photo by Gamma I. Used by permission of the artist.

To gather in the name of Jesus
is to gather with one heart and soul.
What might these people be saying to one another?

A Greeting from the Psalms

Host: How very good and pleasant it is when kindred live together in unity.
(Psalm 133:1)
Group Response: How very good it is.

We are believers!
We are Easter people!

Litany

As believers in Christ we celebrate Easter day.

With one heart and soul.

We are Easter people, who wait at dawn for the risen Christ.

With one heart and soul.

Praise God from whom all blessings flow and praise Christ, God's only Child.

All: With one heart and soul. Alleluia! Amen!

responsive reading

Leader: Believers gathered and told their stories of the resurrection of Christ Jesus.

Believers: The tomb was open. Jesus' body was gone. We were amazed and concerned!

Leader: Believers gathered and shared stories and possessions. Later they went into the world telling the Resurrection story.

Believers: We give testimony when we gather to hear God's Word and to sing God's praises.

Group 1: We give testimony in words. Jesus is our Savior.

Group 2: We give testimony through our actions when we take time to help others.

Group 3: We give testimony when we give money that, combined with the offerings of others, provides for the needy.

Group 4: We give testimony when we honor people of all ages, all races, and all religions.

All Believers: We give testimony when we love and help our neighbors and when we forgive those who hurt us. We give testimony when we turn to God in prayer asking for God's love, God's guidance, and God's forgiveness.

Hine MaTov

Hine MaTov

Words: Psalm 133:1

Music: Israeli round

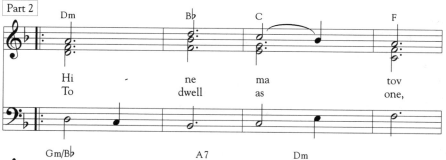

To sing this as a round, divide into two groups. Groups A sings Part 1 twice, then Part 2 twice. Groups B sings Part 1 as Group A sings Part 2.

YOU ARE WITNESSES

Then Jesus opened their minds to understand the scriptures, and said to them, "Thus it is written, that the Messiah is to suffer and to rise from the dead on the third day, and that repentance and forgiveness of sins is to be proclaimed in the Messiah's name to all nations, beginning from Jerusalem. You are witnesses of these things."

Luke 24:45–48

Osmond Watson, *Hallelujah*, 1969, The National Gallery of Jamaica, Kingston, Jamaica. Photograph by Donnette Zacca. Used by permission.

Call to Worship

Person: Thanks be to God.

Leader: We have come to hear a story of God's people.

All: Thanks be to God for the story.

Group 1: We come to hear about God's greatest gift, Jesus.

Group 2: God loved the world so much that God gave and gave, even giving the life of God's only Child.

All: Thanks be to God for the gift of Jesus.

Girls: God would not let Jesus' life end on a cross. On the third day Jesus rose from the dead.

Boys: Jesus, who once lived among us, lives now in our hearts.

All: Thanks be to God for Jesus in our lives.

There are many ways to tell the good news that is in the Gospel. We can shout or sing praise to God. We can proclaim the risen Christ. What might these faces be trying to tell us?

HALELUYA! PELO TSA RONA

Hallelujah! We Sing Your Praises

Words and music: South African

witness...one who sees or has personal knowledge of a fact or event...one who testifies to a fact...to bear testimony or give evidence.

What can I do?

Let Us LOVE

We know love by this, that Jesus laid down life for us—and we ought to lay down our lives for one another. Little children, let us love, not in word or speech, but in truth and action.

1 John 3:16–18

WANTED: Shepherd

In Bible times, the job of shepherd was important. Look at the "job description" list and write a want ad for a good shepherd.
- Care for flocks of sheep and goats night and day.
- Protect flocks from wild enemies such as lions, leopards, wolves, snakes, and scorpions.
- Lead flocks to fresh grazing land and clean water.
- Rescue trapped sheep with staff; fight off wild beasts with wooden club.
- Repay the owner for any stolen sheep.

You Are Mine

1. I will come to you in the silence,
I will lift you from all your fear.
You will hear my voice,
I claim you as my choice,
be still and know I am here.

2. I am hope for all who are hopeless,
I am eyes for all who long to see.
In the shadows of the night,
I will be your light,
come and rest in me.

Refrain
Do not be afraid, I am with you.
I have called you each by name.
Come and follow me,
I will bring you home;
I love you and you are mine.

3. I am strength for all the despairing,
healing for the ones who dwell in shame.
All the blind will see,
the lame will all run free,
and all will know my name.
(Refrain)

4. I am the Word that leads all to freedom,
I am the peace the world cannot give.
I will call your name,
embracing all your pain,
stand up, now walk, and live!
(Refrain)

Maurice Sendak, *In the Dumps* as reproduced in *We Are All in the Dumps with Jack and Guy* (New York: HarperCollins Publishers, 1993). © 1993 by Maurice Sendak. Used by permission of HarperCollins Publishers.

Jack and Guy
Went out in the rye
and they found a little boy
with one black eye.
Come says Jack let's knock him
on the head
No says Guy
Let's buy him some bread
You buy one loaf
And I'll buy two
And we'll bring him up
As other folks do.

Traditional rhyme from Mother Goose, interpreted by Maurice Sendak in *We Are All in the Dumps with Jack and Guy* (New York: HarperCollins Publishers, 1993). © 1993 by Maurice Sendak. Used by permission of HarperCollins Publishers.

The Good Shepherd: A Responsive Reading

Leader: Hear these words of Jesus.

Group 1: I am the good shepherd. The good shepherd lays down his life for the sheep.

Group 2: The hired hand who is not the shepherd and does not own the sheep sees the wolf coming and leaves the sheep and runs away. The wolf snatches them and scatters them.

Leader: Hear the words of Jesus.

Group 1: I am the good shepherd. I know my own, and my own know me.

Group 2: The good shepherd knows each sheep by name. He knows how helpless each one is. He knows they depend on him.

Leader: Hear the words of Jesus.

Group 1: I am the good shepherd. I have other sheep that do not belong to this fold. I must bring them also.

Group 2: The good shepherd looks for other sheep who need his care. He looks for them and tends their needs.

All: So there will be one flock, one shepherd.

Based on John 10:11–16

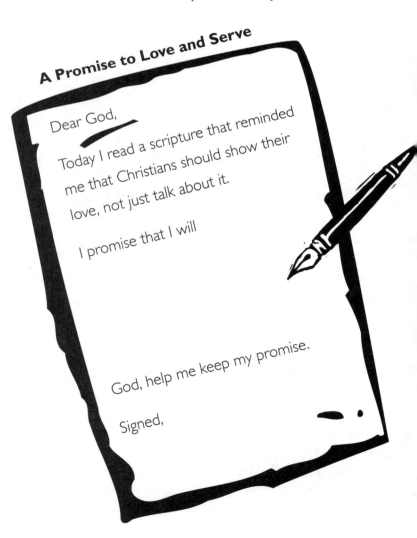

A Promise to Love and Serve

Dear God,

Today I read a scripture that reminded me that Christians should show their love, not just talk about it.

I promise that I will

God, help me keep my promise.

Signed,

Abide in Me

This tree seems to have a center that glows. What might that mean?

Ainslie Roberts, *Laughter at Dawn*, 1976, private collection of Basil Sellars. Used by permission.

I am the vine, you are the branches. Those who abide in me and I in them bear much fruit, because apart from me you can do nothing.

John 15:5

What else can you see that makes this tree different from others?

Why might the painting be called Laughter at Dawn?

Living in Faith

The tree that grows outside my window
is straight and strong and tall.
The mighty winds of winter bend its limbs
and push them to the wall.
But still, it lives.

The tree that grows outside my window
smiles at the springtime sun.
Pale buds burst forth, then leaves, then fruit
splendid with the fragrances of new life.
And still, it lives.

The tree that grows outside my window,
draws strength from deep within the earth,
Where Creator-God, long years ago
provided for its birth.
God planned that it would live.

What of the tree on which I grow?
From where does my strength come?
What holds me fast to truths long told?
And gives me strength to go—
And live, beyond my window?

Dorlis Glass

Jesus, We Want to Meet

Reader 1: Jesus, we want to meet

All: On this thy holy day;

Reader 2: We gather round thy throne

All: On this thy holy day.

Reader 3: We kneel in awe and fear,

All: On this thy holy day.

Reader 4: Pray God to teach us to hear

All: On this thy holy day.

Reader 5: Thy blessing, Lord, we seek,

All: On this thy holy day;

Readers 1 & 2: Give joy of thy victory

All: On this thy holy day.

Readers 3 & 4: Our minds we dedicate

All: On this thy holy day;

Reader 5: Heart and soul consecrate

All: On this thy holy day.

A. T. Olajida Olude, 1949; translated by Bieodun Adebesin; versed by Austin C. Lovelace, 1962. Abingdon Press 1964. Used by permission.

This is an icon called the *Tree of Life.*

The face of Jesus shines at the center of the cross to remind us that Jesus is the center of creation. What about this icon might remind you of today's scripture reading?

Robert Lentz, *Tree of Life*,
Bridge Building Images,
Burlington, Vermont.
Used by permission.

Sing a New Song

Georges Seurat, *Bathers at Asnières*, detail, The National Gallery, London, England (Erich Lessing/Art Resource, N.Y.). Used by permission.

O sing to God a new song. God has remembered God's steadfast love and faithfulness to the house of Israel. All the ends of the earth have seen the victory of our God.

Psalm 98:1a, 3

Have you ever had a song in your head you just had to sing? What a joy to open your mouth and sing praise to God.

Litany of Praise and Thanksgiving

Boys: People on earth sing praise, sing to God with a happy voice.
All: Come, sing praise to God.
Girls: Praise, and always sing to God, making joyful noises and singing new songs.
All: Sing for God is good.
God's mercy is forever sure.

Here's a *New Song*
(Sing to "She'll Be Coming 'round the Mountain")

Clap your hands, all you people, clap your hands!
Clap your hands, all you people, clap your hands!
Clap your hands, all you people!
Clap your hands, all you people, clap your hands!
All you people, clap your hands!

Anonymous

Unison Benediction

As God has loved me,
I have loved you;
abide in my love.
I have said these
things to you so that
my joy may be in you,
and that your joy may
be complete.

John 15:9, 11

God of the Sparrow God of the Whale

Words: Jaroslav J. Vajda, 1983

Tune: ROEDER 5.4.6.7.7.
Carl F. Schalk, 1983

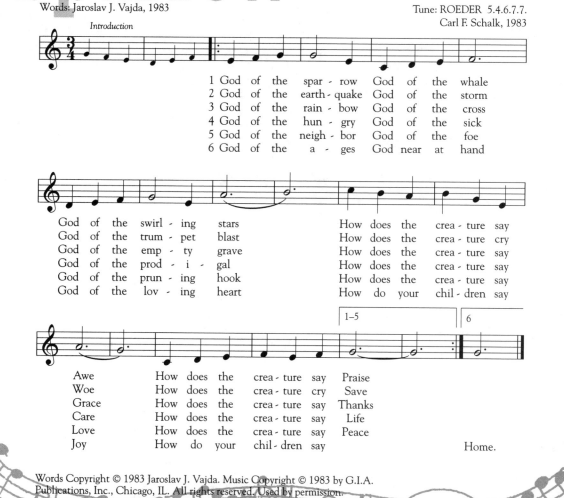

1 God of the spar-row God of the whale
2 God of the earth-quake God of the storm
3 God of the rain-bow God of the cross
4 God of the hun-gry God of the sick
5 God of the neigh-bor God of the foe
6 God of the a-ges God near at hand

God of the swirl-ing stars   How does the crea-ture say
God of the trum-pet blast   How does the crea-ture cry
God of the emp-ty grave   How does the crea-ture say
God of the prod-i-gal   How does the crea-ture say
God of the prun-ing hook   How does the crea-ture say
God of the lov-ing heart   How do your chil-dren say

1–5   6

Awe   How does the crea-ture say   Praise
Woe   How does the crea-ture cry   Save
Grace   How does the crea-ture say   Thanks
Care   How does the crea-ture say   Life
Love   How does the crea-ture say   Peace
Joy   How do your chil-dren say   Home.

That They May Be One

George Tooker, *Embrace of Peace*, Hartland, Vermont. Used by permission of the artist.

Look at the faces of these people.

Might they be at peace?

What, if anything, about this painting might make you think of peace?

Jesus said, "I am no longer in the world, but they are in the world, and I am coming to you. Holy God, Father and Mother, protect them in your name that you have given me, so that they may be one, as we are one."

John 17:11

CALL TO WORSHIP

Boys: Happy are you who find joy in obeying the law of God.

Girls: Happy are those who think about it day and night.

Boys: They are like trees that grow beside a stream that bear fruit in season. Their leaves do not wither.

Girls: They succeed in everything they do.

All: The righteous are guided and protected by God.

Paraphrase of Psalm 1:1a, 2–4, 6a

A Mystery

A boy stood on a shore and threw a pebble into the lake. With a splash it set into motion a series of circles that radiated out from the point where the pebble hit. The boy watched and wondered. How could it be? How could one small pebble make the whole surface of the lake come alive?

God sent God's only Child into the world. God wanted all of creation to know how much God loved them. God wanted the relationship between God and God's people to go on and on—into eternity. The Child grew and told God's story. Those who heard told it too. How could one child, just one person, cause such a stir in history?

The Child sent those he loved into the world with a purpose. The Child wanted all of creation to know how much God loved them. The Child wanted all creation to live eternally with God. Those who loved the Child told the story. They told it again and again. They told it to their families, to their neighbors, and even to strangers. How could they have changed the lives of so many?

The symbol of the cross, orb, and crown

is based on the ancient symbol known as the Cross of Victory, or the Cross Triumphant. This symbol is made up of a crown on top of a cross, all on top of an orb or globe. This symbolizes the reign of the risen Christ over all the world. The orb, representing the world, reminds believers of the command Christ gave the disciples: "You shall be my witnesses in Jerusalem and in all Judea and Samaria and to the end of the earth."

All May Be One, United Church of Christ Headquarters, Cleveland, Ohio. Used by permission.

The Spirit helps us in our weakness; for we do not know how to pray as we ought, but that very Spirit intercedes with sighs too deep for words.

Romans 8:26

Spirit of Comfort

Beauford Delaney, *Can Fire in the Park, detail* 1946, National Museum of American Art, Washington, D.C. (National Museum of American Art, Washington D.C./ Art Resource, N.Y.). Used by permission.

Where What does the fire in this painting remind you of?

might you want to be if you were in this scene?

In what ways might the picture reflect warmth and comfort?

What might the Spirit say through me?

Write down how you might respond to each situation if the Spirit was speaking through you.

You meet a sixth grader whose house was lost in a flood

_____

You talk with a very old woman who is all alone in the world

_____

You hear that your best friend's parents are getting a divorce

_____

Soplo de Dios viviente

Osvaldo Catena; alt.
Transl. *The New Century Hymnal*

Music: Norwegian traditional melody
Arranged by Lorraine Floríndez, 1991

1 So - plo de Dios vi - vien - te que en el prin - ci - pio cu - bris - te el a - gua;
1 Breath of the liv - ing God, who in the be - gin - ning moved o'er the wa - ters,
2 Breath of the liv - ing God, whose e - ter - nal Word came to dwell a - mong us,

So - plo de Dios vi - vien - te que fe - cun - das - te la cre - a - ción.
Breath of the liv - ing God, by whom all cre - a - tion was first con - ceived;
Breath of the liv - ing God, by whom all cre - a - tion has been re - newed;

Estribillo (Refrain)

¡Ven hoy a nues - tras vi - das in - fún - de - nos tus do - nes,
Come now and live with - in us, come, let your gifts en - rich us,

So - plo de Dios vi - vien - te, oh San - to Es - pí - ri - tu Cre - a - dor!
Breath of the liv - ing God, our Cre - a - tor Spir - it, e - ter - nal Source.

In the year that King Uzziah died, I saw God sitting on a throne, high and lofty. A seraph called to another and said: "Holy, holy, holy is the God of hosts; the whole earth is full of God's glory."

Isaiah 6:1a, 3

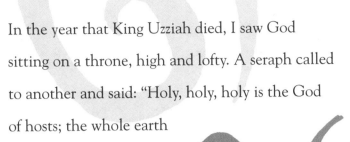

Holy, HOLY, Holy Holy

Manuscript illumination, *The Vision of Isaiah*, c. 1000, Staatsbibliothek, Bamberg, Germany. Used by permission.

*S*eraphs have three pairs of wings. How many seraphs do you see in this art?

*R*ead Isaiah 6:1–8. How many things named in these verses do you see in this art?

*L*ook at the animals in the circles in each corner. Why do you think the artist selected these animals?

Eula McCloud *(far left)*

Whom shall I send?

Kate Goodspeed responded when the Amity Foundation asked for an English teacher to be sent to the Nanjing Institute of Architecture and Civil Engineering in Nanjing, China. "My students are wonderful," she wrote. "Tonight I sat with candles, cokes and fruit (provided by the students) and cookies, an *Ebony* magazine (very popular!) and a family photo album in a dorm room shared by eight students, all of them clustered around, eyes shining in the candlelight, struggling to find the English phrases to talk to me. I am their first foreign teacher."

Eula McCloud has been cook at The Carolinian, a United Church of Christ-related retirement home owned by the Retirement Housing Foundation in Florence, South Carolina. She goes out of her way to give special care to the residents— preparing favorite dishes, bringing flowers when they are ill, doing all she can to brighten their days.

Hospitality is a key to the ministry of Wallace and Ruth Robeson, who have been missionaries in Turkey for over forty years. Wallace teaches English reading at the University of the Aegean, and is the warden at St. John's Anglican Church, which they attend. Ruth organizes the congregation's potluck suppers, hosts the many friends and guests who pass through Izmir, and works with a group of Turkish women learning conversational English.

Here I am, send me!

Ed and Robbie Doughty of Norway, Maine, have found their way to Honduras almost every winter since 1970. Since their family camping area was a summer business, they were able to devote their winter months as volunteers assisting Dr. Joyce Baker in her mission and ministry in rural clinics in Honduras. Ed performed carpentry, plumbing, and electrical chores, and he built and renovated buildings. Robbie answered correspondence, sorted and organized medical supplies, and did general office administrative tasks.

Ed *and* **Robbie Doughty**

These people answered God's call with "Here I am; send me." What might God be calling you to do?

The stories on this page are reprinted by permission from *In Mission 1994/1995: A Calendar of Prayer for the United Church of Christ* (October 25, September 19, June 3, and February 2) published by the United Church Board for Homeland Ministries and the United Church Board for World Ministries, Cleveland, Ohio.

Ben Shahn, *Beatitude*, 1952, private collection. Used by permission of VAGA.

On the Sabbath?

Have you ever seen a field of ripe grain swaying in the wind?

When the sun shines on it, the heads of grain look golden.

One sabbath Jesus was going through the grainfields; and as they made their way the disciples began to pluck heads of grain. The Pharisees said to Jesus, "Look, why are they doing what is not lawful on the sabbath?"

Mark 2:23–24

93

Sopla de Dios viviente
Breath of the Living God

Rules and laws are important and must be enforced strictly to have order in our society.

Rules and laws are not important because people should be free to do as they please.

Jesus said to them, "The sabbath was made for humankind, and not humankind for the sabbath."

Osvaldo Catena; alt.
Transl. *The New Century Hymnal*

Music: Norwegian traditional melody
Arranged by Lorraine Floríndez, 1991

1 So - plo de Dios vi - vien - te que en el prin - ci - pio cu - bris - te el a - gua;
1 Breath of the liv - ing God, who in the be - gin - ning moved o'er the wa - ters,
2 Breath of the liv - ing God, whose e - ter - nal Word came to dwell a - mong us,

So - plo de Dios vi - vien - te que fe - cun - das - te la cre - a - ción.
Breath of the liv - ing God, by whom all cre - a - tion was first con - ceived;
Breath of the liv - ing God, by whom all cre - a - tion has been re - newed;

Estribillo (Refrain)

¡Ven hoy a nues - tras vi - das in - fún - de - nos tus do - nes,
Come now and live with - in us, come, let your gifts en - rich us,

So - plo de Dios vi - vien - te, oh San - to Es - pí - ri - tu Cre - a - dor!
Breath of the liv - ing God, our Cre - a - tor Spir - it, e - ter - nal Source.

We know that if the earthly tent we live in is destroyed, we have a building from God, a house not made with hands, eternal in the heavens.

2 Corinthians 5:1

The Eternal

Christo and Jeanne-Claude, *Running Fence, Sonoma and Marin Counties, California, 1972–1976.* © Christo, 1976, photo by Jeanne-Claude. Used by permission of the artists.

What do you notice about this fence in California?

Would you like to have to paint or whitewash this fence? Why or why not?

Can you see the end of the fence?

where?

why? what?

Show Us the Way

O God my God

O God our redeemer

show us the way

to a new life

where there is no hate and bigotry

show us the method

of ending our oppression

by nonviolence and love

show us how to struggle

   O God

show us the way to thee

we shall clearly see thy way

and follow thee into eternity.

Benjamin F. Chavis, Jr., *Psalms from Prison*
(Cleveland, Ohio: The Pilgrim Press, 1994).
Used by permission.

During this week, be alert for ways you and your family can bring hope for today and the future to someone.

Watch for signs of hopelessness in your neighborhood, your community, on television, and in the newspaper.

Together, find a way to lessen the suffering of someone, offering that person the hope of the eternal.

Live by Faith

So we are always confident;
for we walk by faith, not by sight.

2 Corinthians 5:6a, 7

O Holy God, we live in a world that can be confusing and scary. When we feel that way, we look all around us to find something in which we can put our trust. Sometimes nothing is there. It is at those times, O God, that in confidence we reach out to you. Thank you for always being there when we need you. Amen.

Ethan Hubbard, *Sisters in the Wind,* as reproduced in Ethan Hubbard, *Staight to the Heart: Children of the World* (Chelsea, Vt.: Craftsbury Common Books, 1992). Used by permission of the photographer.

What about the two sisters in this photograph suggests faith to you? How does the photograph connect with the Bible verse for today? with the prayer on this page?

Live by Faith

Read the following stories. Decide how each person could live out his or her faith by showing love to some other person.

Write your ending on the blank lines.

Gerald had seen the new boy eating alone for several days. Today he had learned that José and his mother had come to the city after José's father died. His mother wanted to be closer to José's grandparents. Once again, as he came into the school cafeteria, he saw José at a table all by himself, so

....

....

Marsha had looked forward to Natasha's birthday party for weeks. It was going to be her first night party. She had even persuaded her mom to let her buy a new outfit. At 5:00 she was all dressed and waiting for her mother to come home from work to drive her to Natasha's house. At 5:15 the phone rang.

"I'm at the emergency room at the hospital," her mother said. "Aunt Betty had a stroke. I know you are supposed to go to Natasha's party, but I need you to watch your little sister until I can get home. No one else is here with Aunt Betty. I'll get home when I can."

"Mom," Marsha said, "..

....

.... "

Jamal and Todd sat on the front porch and watched Mr. Skillern trying to plant flowers in his yard. Mr. Skillern walked with a cane, so he was having a hard time. The boys did not like Mr. Skillern. He complained to their parents that they messed up his flower beds playing ball.

"Look at Mr. Skillern," Todd said. "He is going to fall down in his precious flowers, and I'm going to laugh!"

"Yes," Jamal said. "I think ....

....

.... "

98

David and Goliath

Can you think of a Bible story that this picture might illustrate?

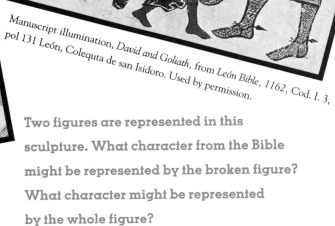

Manuscript illumination, *David and Goliath*, from *León Bible*, 1162, Cod. I. 3, pol 131 León, Colequta de san Isidoro. Used by permission.

Jean Ipoustéguy, *David and Goliath*, 1959, The Museum of Modern Art, New York, N.Y. Used by permission.

Two figures are represented in this sculpture. What character from the Bible might be represented by the broken figure? What character might be represented by the whole figure?

But David said to the Philistine, "You come to me with sword and spear and javelin; but I come to you in the name of the God of hosts. This very day God will deliver you into my hand."

1 Samuel 17:45a, 46a

Litany

God is strong for those who are weak.

God helps people in times of trouble.

Those who know God, trust God.

Sing praise to God.

All: Tell all the peoples what God has done.

Paraphrase of Psalm 9:9–11

99

God's strength helps all people do impossible things.

Photographs by Evan Golder and Steve Bigby, *Sandbagging the Mississippi River*, 1993, St. Louis, Missouri. Used by permission of the Office of Communication, United Church of Christ.

Thuma Mina
Send Me Now

South African traditional song

Leader · All

1 Thu - ma mi - na.   1 Thu - ma mi - na, thu - ma mi - na,
1 Send me, Je - sus, send me, Je - sus,
2 Lead me, Je - sus, lead me, Je - sus,
3 Fill me, Je - sus, fill me, Je - sus,

1–2 · 3

Thu - ma mi - na, So - man - dla.
Send me, Je - sus, send me now.
Lead me, Je - sus, lead me now.
Fill me, Je - sus, fill me now.

Leader
1 Send me now.
2 Lead me now.
3 Fill me now.

If I could talk to each youngster in the United States, I would have one message to give them. I would say, **"You are important to the world. You are needed. Most of all, you can make a difference in someone else's life.** Begin by doing something that shows you care. That's where satisfaction in life begins. And if one day you get a feeling that says you can change the world, trust that feeling. Because *you* make a difference. There is something important that needs to happen in the world because of you, and it *can* happen if you do it."

Mary Conway Kohler, *Young People Learning to Care* (New York: The Seabury Press), 9.

Generous Acts

The gift is acceptable according to what one has—not according to what one does not have.

2 Corinthians 8:12b

Clara McBride Hale's

long career caring for sick children began in 1969 when a young woman appeared at her door with a drug-addicted baby. Before her death at age 87 in 1992, Mother Hale was a foster-care mother for more than four decades. She also founded Hale House, a safe, loving environment that has nurtured more than 1,000 young victims of New York City's drug and AIDS epidemics.

Stephen Shames/Matrix, *Mother Clara Hale at 87*, as reproduced in *The African Americans* (New York: Penguin Books, 1993). Used by permission of Matrix International, Inc.

Mother Hale responded in love to the needs of people around her. What can you do to respond to the needs of the people who live around you?

Stewardship Litany

Because you give us food to eat,
We give ourselves to you, O God!
Because you give us clothes to wear,
We give ourselves to you, O God!
Because you give us money to spend,
We give our money and ourselves to you, O God.
Because you give us people who care about us,
We give ourselves to you, O God!
In response to all that you do for us and give to us,
We give ourselves to you, O God!

Prayer

• • •

Gracious and giving God, help us to remember all that you have given us and to share those gifts with others. Remind us to open our hearts to all people who are in need of our help.

Amen.

I will give my gifts from God

I will give my talent,
my song,
my hands,
my willing heart.
I will give my fortune,
my pennies,
my food,
my open home.
I will give in the name of Jesus,
all that I have,
all that I own,
because they are all gifts from God.

Sent by Jesus

Jesus called the twelve and began to send them out two by two, and gave them authority over the unclean spirits. Jesus ordered them to take nothing for their journey except a staff.

Mark 6:7–8a

Sent by Jesus, Vie de Jesus Mafa, 24 rue du Marechal Joffre, 78000 Versailles, France. All rights reserved. Used by permission.

A mission journey is about to begin. Where might these people be going?

What might their mission be? If you were one of these people,

which one might you be?

Litany

Jesus has called us.
Where might we go?
Jesus is with us.
What shall we do?
Jesus is leading us.
Our journey is about to begin.
All: Jesus stay at our side.

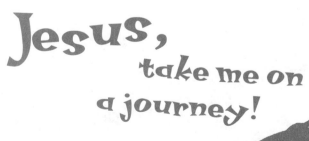

Jesus, take me on a journey!

WANTED!
A FEW GOOD SINGERS

WHAT: TO JOIN THE CHOIR
WHEN: REHEARSALS FROM
7:30–9:00 P.M. ON WEDNESDAYS
SING EACH SUNDAY FOR WORSHIP FROM
10:30–11:30 A.M.
NO EXPERIENCE NECESSARY!

WANTED!
DUSTERS, SWEEPERS, POLISHERS

WHAT: TO CLEAN CHURCH BUILDING
WHEN: SATURDAYS EACH WEEK
APPLY TODAY!

Thuma Mina
Send Me Now

South African traditional song

1 Thu - ma mi - na. | 1 Thu - ma mi - na, thu - ma mi - na,
1 Send me, Je - sus, send me, Je - sus,
2 Lead me, Je - sus, lead me, Je - sus,
3 Fill me, Je - sus, fill me, Je - sus,

Thu - ma mi - na, So - man - dla. | 1 Send me now.
Send me, Je - sus, send me now. | 2 Lead me now.
Lead me, Je - sus, lead me now. | 3 Fill me now.
Fill me, Je - sus, fill me now.

When the journey seems long and the mission impossible, remember the love of Jesus is with you.

Dance before God

David and all
the house of Israel
were dancing before
God with all their
might, with songs
and lyres and harps
and tambourines and
castanets and cymbals.

2 Samuel 6:5

Black Feet Indian Reservation, Tony Stone Images, Chicago, Illinois, Used by permission.

Litany

I will dance with joy,

For God is my savior.

I will sing and dance while giggling,

For God has been good to me.

I will dance and shout with laugher,

For God has smiled at me.

*All: God is great, God is good,
and God loves me.*

**Dance may express many different things.
What might this dance be expressing?**

105

Drums: Make a drum out of a large coffee can, or a round box such as an oatmeal box. The drum could be played with your hands, or with sticks or pencils. You could also make a drum by turning an empty wastepaper basket upside down.

Tambourines: Make a tambourine out of two metal or plastic pie plates by stapling or taping them together with the insides facing each other. Clappers could be added by stapling yarn strung with buttons to the outside edge of the plates.

Shakers: Make shakers by filling small boxes or plastic jars with sand, salt, rice, dried beans, small stones, or other materials that will make noise when the boxes or jars are shaken.

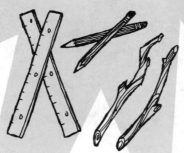

Rhythm sticks: Make rhythm sticks from pencils, rulers, or twigs. All you need are two long objects that will make a noise when struck together.

Rhythm Poem

Sing and dance,
dance and shout!
(yell and clap)
Praise God with movement,
move all about!
(stand and shake)
Sing and dance,
dance and spin!
(move and spin)
Praise God with leaping,
let the Spirit in!
(move and play instruments)

God is the dance
—and the dance goes on—
rejoice!

Christ has abolished the law with its commandments and ordinances, in order to create in Christ one new humanity in place of the two, thus making peace, and in order to reconcile both groups to God in one body through the cross.

Ephesians 2:15–16a

IN ONE BODY

The Wall Came Tumbling Down (New York: Arch Cape Press, 1990), 58.
Used by permission of AP/Wide World Photos.

A long time ago, before you were born, people built a wall in the town of Berlin that divided both sides of the city and separated friends and family. The wall was built because people had differences. In 1991 the Berlin Wall came down. The people rejoiced. Can you think of a time when you might have been glad to see friends and family brought together again?

Do's and Don'ts

Do take down walls — Don't build them!

Do knock down fences — Don't raise them!

Do work to make God's family a united one — Don't leave anyone out!

LET US BECOME ONE . . .

ONE BODY IN CHRIST

We Are Your People

Words: Brian Wren, 1973; rev. 1993

Music: John Wilson, 1973

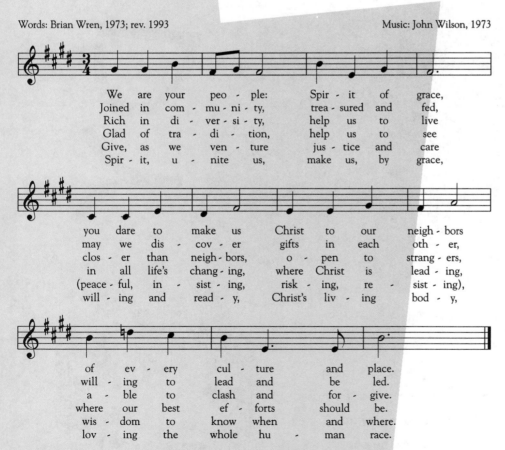

We are your peo - ple: Spir - it of grace,
Joined in com - mu - ni - ty, trea - sured and fed,
Rich in di - ver - si - ty, help us to live
Glad of tra - di - tion, help us to see
Give, as we ven - ture jus - tice and care
Spir - it, u - nite us, make us, by grace,

you dare to make us Christ to our neigh - bors
may we dis - cov - er gifts in each oth - er,
clos - er than neigh - bors, o - pen to strang - ers,
in all life's chang - ing, where Christ is lead - ing,
(peace - ful, in - sist - ing, risk - ing, re - sist - ing),
will - ing and read - y, Christ's liv - ing bod - y,

of ev - ery cul - ture and place.
will - ing to lead and be led.
a - ble to clash and for - give.
where our best ef - forts should be.
wis - dom to know when and where.
lov - ing the whole hu - man race.

Prayer

God who gave us all we see, who made us one big family, help us to make ourselves into one "body" of your children. Amen.

Five Thousand Fed

One of Jesus' disciples, Andrew, Simon Peter's brother, said to him, "There is a boy here who has five barley loaves and two fish. But what are they among so many people?" Then Jesus took the loaves, and when he had given thanks, he distributed them to those who were seated; so also the fish, as much as they wanted.

John 6:8–9, 11

Litany

Group 1: Come to the feast.

Group 2: The table is spread.

Group 3: There are fishes and bread.

Group 1: Come to the hillside, the feast is ready.

Group 2: But the fishes are two.

Group 3: And the bread slices few.

Group 1: But Jesus has called us.

Group 2: He breaks now the bread.

Group 3: Jesus, Messiah, the multitude fed.

All: Jesus we know you are great!

Alemayehu Bizuneh, *Scene X of the Misereor "Hunger Cloth" from Ethiopia*, Aachen, Germany. Used by permission of Misereor Medienproduktion und Vertriebsbesellschaft mbH.

Imagine you are one of the people in this picture. Who might you be?

An Acrostic Poem

Lots of people,
Old and young,
All wanted to hear Jesus.
Very late it got,
Everyone was hungry.
So many to feed.

Fish, just two, and loaves, just five . . .
Into Jesus' hands they went.
Surprised me and all my friends!
Hungry we no longer were, but satisfied.

Haleluya! Pelo tsa rona
Halleluya! We Sing Your Praises

Words and music: South African

Refrain

Ha - le - lu - ya! Pe - lo tsa ro - na, di tha - bi - le ka - o - fe -
Hal - le - lu - ya! We sing your prais - es, all our hearts with glad - ness are

la. Ha - le - lu - ya! Pe - lo tsa ro - na, di tha - bi - le ka - o - fe -
filled. Hal - le - lu - ya! We sing your prais - es, all our hearts with glad - ness are

Last time, end Stanzas

la. 1 Ke Mo - re - na Je - so, ya re du - me - let - seng,
filled. 1 Je - sus Christ said to us: I am wine, I am bread,
2 Christ now sends us all out, strong in faith, free of doubt;

To Refrain

ya re du - me - let - seng, ho tsa - mai - sa e - van - ge - di.
I am wine, I am bread, give to all who hun - ger and thirst.
strong in faith, free of doubt; tell to all the joy - ful Good News.

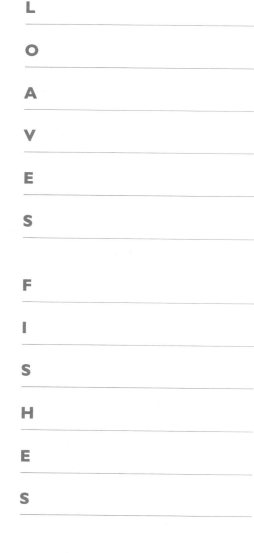

L
O
A
V
E
S

F
I
S
H
E
S

Jacopo Bassano, *Feeding of the Five Thousand*,
Earl Spencer Collection, Althorp, Northants,
Great Britain (Bridgeman/Art Resource, N.Y.).
Used by permission.

GROWING
in Christ

But speaking the truth in love, we must grow up in every way into the one who is the head, into Christ.

Ephesians 4:15

Rembrandt Harmensz van Rijn, *The Apostle Paul in Prison*, Staatsgalerie, Stuttgart, Germany (Foto Marburg/Art Resource, N.Y.). Used by permission.

HELP WANTED

Immediate opening available for newly created position of apostle.

Must _____

_____

_____

_____

_____

_____

_____

Imagine what a help wanted ad for an apostle might have said to attract the apostle Paul's attention.

111

Words: Brian Wren, 1973; rev. 1993   Music: John Wilson, 1973

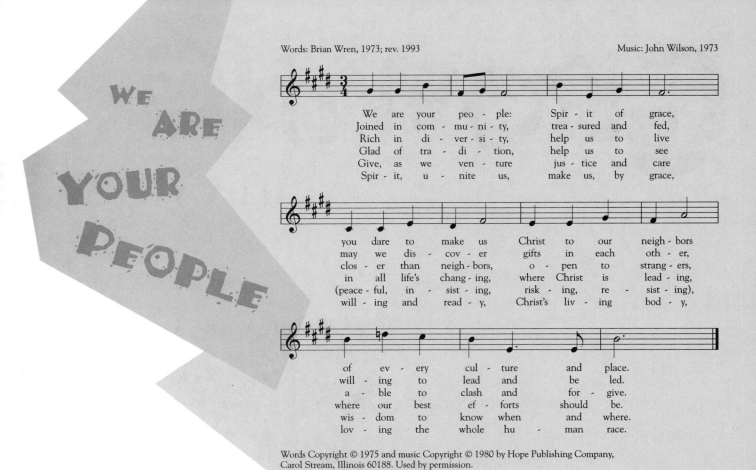

WE ARE YOUR PEOPLE

We are your peo - ple: Spir - it of grace,
Joined in com - mu - ni - ty, trea - sured and fed,
Rich in di - ver - si - ty, help us to live
Glad of tra - di - tion, help us to see
Give, as we ven - ture jus - tice and care
Spir - it, u - nite us, make us, by grace,

you dare to make us Christ to our neigh - bors
may we dis - cov - er gifts in each oth - er,
clos - er than neigh - bors, o - pen to strang - ers,
in all life's chang - ing, where Christ is lead - ing,
(peace - ful, in - sist - ing, risk - ing, re - sist - ing),
will - ing and read - y, Christ's liv - ing bod - y,

of ev - ery cul - ture and place.
will - ing to lead and be led.
a - ble to clash and for - give.
where our best ef - forts should be.
wis - dom to know when and where.
lov - ing the whole hu - man race.

Growing in Christ

A Responsive Reading Based on Ephesians 2:11–22 and 4:1–16

Voice 1: We know that in Christ, hostilities and barriers are broken down;

Voice 2: That in Christ's body, broken in the cross, there is peace.

All: We are part of the body, and we are growing in Christ.

Voice 3: It is up to us to lead a life worthy of the calling to which we have been called.

Voice 4: We must learn to live with all humility and gentleness;

Voice 5: With all patience, making every effort to maintain the unity of the Spirit in peace.

All: We are part of the body, and we are growing in Christ.

Voice 6: Every one of us is called by God to be part of the body of Christ.

Voice 7: We are each different individuals, but together we are made one in Christ.

All: We are part of the body, and we are growing in Christ.

Voice 8: Every single one of us is given gifts by God.

Voice 9: God gives us these gifts so that we can help equip the people of God for daily ministry that builds up and strengthens the body of Christ.

All: We are part of the body and we are growing up into Christ. We have the gifts God has given us, and we intend to use them well.

Grow up and grow strong in Christ!

Touch of an AnGel

Then Elijah lay down under the broom tree and fell asleep. Suddenly an angel touched him and said to him, "Get up and eat." He looked, and there at his head was a cake baked on hot stones and a jar of water.

1 Kings 19:5–6a

Dieric Bouts, *Elijah and the Angel*, Altar of the Last Supper, Collegiale, St. Pierre, Louvain, Belgium (Erich Lessing/Art Resource, N.Y.). Used by permission.

There, in the wilderness, a weary person slept. Ever so gently an angel bent down to touch his shoulder. What do you think the touch of an angel might feel like?

Litany of an Angel

Silently, gently an angel comes near.

God sends an angel.

When we are tired or lonely, the angels appear.

God sends an angel.

The angels are messengers, no one need fear.

God sends an angel.

God sends us love in the touch of an angel
to heal our despair.

All: God's angels are with us. Praise God.

113

prayer

Dear God, come to us when we call your name.

Come to us when we sleep.

Come to us in the brightness of day,

and in the quiet dark of night.

Come to us in our sadness and in our joy.

Come to us, your children, we pray. Amen.

God Is Near

When we are frightened,

God knows our fear.

When we are crying,

God sees our tears.

When we are listening,

God's hope fills our ears.

While we are waiting,

God plans out our years.

When we are laughing,

God's heart feels our cheer.

When we are praying,

Our wishes God hears.

D. GOLDSMITH 96

Fill in the Blank

If an angel touched me I might _____.

Seeking God's Purpose

Solomon prayed, "Give your servant therefore an understanding mind to govern your people, able to discern between good and evil; for who can govern this your great people?"

1 Kings 3:9

This boy has paused for a moment of prayer. When do you pray? What do you talk to God about?

Jeffery Allan Salter, *Taurian Osborne Prays at the New Fellowship Missionary Baptist Church, Opa Laka, Florida.* Used by permission of the photographer.

To be wise— trust God!

God shows the way.

Know God— know life!

Litany of Wisdom

O God, make me wise,

So that I may know how to live.

O God, open my eyes,

So I can help others.

O God, let me follow your ways,

So I may serve you.

All: O God, I will sing your praise.

Dear God,
I want to know
what you want
for me...

A Simple POEM

Smart, I want to be smart.

I want to know,

yes I do,

what's expected of me.

Wise, I want to be wise.

I want to be,

yes I do,

the best I can be.

Draw yourself at prayer and write your request to God in the bubble

Henri Matisse, *The Chapel of the Rosary of the Dominicans, Vence, France.*
Photo by Hélène Adant. Used by permission of Soeur Jacques Marie,
Chapelle de Vence.

Imagine stepping into this worship space. What might it be like to put your bare feet on the cool marble floor or to listen to the quiet and watch the sunlight dance on the walls. Do you think God might be in this place?

The Dwelling Place

Then Solomon stood before the altar of God in the presence of all the assembly of Israel, and spread out his hands to heaven: "Hear the plea of your servant and of your people Israel when they pray toward this place; O hear in heaven your dwelling place; heed and forgive."

1 Kings 8:22, 30

Litany

Come, O God, our Creator.

We praise your name.

Come into the place where we gather.

We praise your name.

Come into our hearts, our minds, our lives.

We praise your name.

All: God is to be worshiped in this place.

Prayer

Dear God, open us to all the sacred spaces and places where we might worship you. We praise your holy name. Amen.

Here, where a church once stood, stands a window in ruins. There is only the arch and the wonderful view of the ocean. People once worshiped God in this place. How might God be worshiped here today?

Look all around, at all the spaces and in all the places for God—and worship God there!

118

Doers of the word

But be doers of the word, and not merely hearers who deceive themselves.

James 1:22

Don't just listen . . . do something in the name of God!

Alan S. Weiner/NYT Pictures, *Oseola McCarty*. Used by permission.

This woman gave all the money she earned so that some young people might have financial help going to college. Why do you think a person might do something like that?

Choral Reading

Let everyone be quick to hear.

(Action: Tilt head to one side and place a cupped hand to the ear.)

Let everyone be slow to speak.

(Action: Place finger to closed lips.)

Let everyone be slow to anger.

(Action: Sit down and cross arms over chest in a resting position.)

Let everyone be doers of the Word.

(Action: Jump up and stretch out arms as if ready to receive something.)

Prayer of Dedication

Gracious God, you are a God of action. You do more than watch us from a long way off; you are a part of our lives every day. Help us to be a people of action, to be "doers of your word." Be with us during the week and remind us of the people we learned about today who were doers of the Word. We have made these signs to be active in your world. Bless them and our work, for we wish to be doers of the Word. Amen.